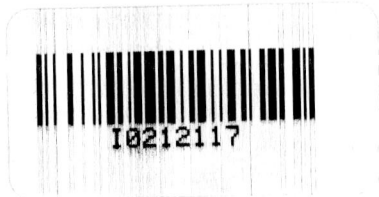

FINDING YOURSELF

AFTER DIVORCE

Reclaim Your Power, Rediscover Your Joy, and
Rewrite the Rest of Your Life

by

Sophia Lane

Copyright 2025 Sophia Lane.
All rights reserved.

No part of this book may be reproduced in any form or by any electronic or mechanical means including information storage and retrieval systems, without permission in writing from the author. The only exception is by a reviewer, who may quote short excerpts in a review.

Although the author and publisher have made every effort to ensure that the information in this book was correct at press time, the author and publisher do not assume and hereby disclaim any liability to any party for any loss, damage, or disruption caused by errors or omissions, whether such errors or omissions result from negligence, accident, or any other cause.

This publication is designed to provide accurate and authoritative information with regard to the subject matter covered. It is sold with the understanding that the publisher is not engaged in rendering professional services. If legal advice or other expert assistance is required, the services of a competent professional should be sought.

The fact that an organization or website is referred to in this work as a citation and/or a potential source of further information does not mean that the author or the publisher endorses the information the organization or website may provide or recommendations it may make.

Please remember that Internet websites listed in this work may have changed or disappeared between when this work was written and when it is read.

Finding Yourself After Divorce : Reclaim
Your Power, Rediscover Your Joy, and
Rewrite the Rest of Your Life

TABLE OF CONTENTS

INTRODUCTION

Divorce marks a significant turning point, often stirring a whirlwind of emotions and uncertainties. For many, it feels like standing at the edge of a vast, unfamiliar landscape—one that's both intimidating and filled with potential. You may find yourself grappling with feelings of loss, confusion, even relief, all tangled together. This moment, while incredibly challenging, also holds the promise of new beginnings and self-discovery. The journey after divorce isn't about forgetting what came before but about learning how to build something fresh and meaningful for yourself.

It's common to feel like you're navigating without a map—unsure where to turn or what step to take next. That's why this book is designed as a supportive guide, offering encouragement and practical advice for moving forward with strength and hope. The path through post-divorce life isn't linear. You might bump into old feelings, face setbacks, or question your worth along the way. But you don't have to go through it alone, and there's absolutely no need to rush the healing process. Every emotion you feel is valid, and every step you take is progress.

Behind the pain, there's a core truth that often goes unspoken: divorce doesn't define who you are. It might feel like a loss of identity, especially if you linked much of your sense of self to the marriage. But the reality is that you are more than that relationship. This moment in your life presents a unique chance to reconnect with who you truly are, apart from the roles and expectations that may have weighed you down. Rebuilding confidence and a solid sense of self is not only possible—it's essential to thriving after divorce.

Many people carry unnecessary shame or guilt when a marriage ends, often feeling as if they somehow failed. Society's old narratives about divorce can make you question your worth or blame yourself for things beyond your control. It's important to recognize these feelings for what they are: cultural baggage that no longer serves you. Embracing self-compassion and shedding those harmful beliefs can lighten your emotional load and open the door to genuine healing.

This introduction invites you to look forward with an open heart and mind. It's about understanding that endings also bring new chances—to redefine your purpose, to dream without limits, and to nurture the person you've always been underneath it all. Healing is neither quick nor easy, but it is within your reach. You will find ways to reclaim joy, establish emotional independence, and reconnect with your passions and values. With the right mindset and tools, you can transform the hardship of divorce into a powerful catalyst for personal reinvention.

Moving forward after divorce means learning how to let go of the past without erasing it. It requires patience, kindness, and sometimes a willingness to seek support when things get tough. But it also means celebrating the inner strength that got you through the hardest moments. You may surprise yourself with just how resilient you are. This book will walk alongside you as you build new rituals and routines, find your voice again, and begin to trust your own decisions. Every chapter is crafted to empower you step by step, helping you reclaim your life on your terms.

It's perfectly natural to face a mix of emotions, sometimes conflicting and overwhelming. You might feel liberated one day and deeply sad the next. That's part of the process. Healing isn't about pushing feelings aside— it's about honoring them, understanding where they come from, and gently releasing what no longer serves you. Grief, anger, relief, hope—they all have a place in your journey. Recognizing this complexity is a key part of moving forward with clarity and compassion.

As you read further, you'll find encouragement to explore who you are beyond the divorce. What dreams did you put on hold? What parts of yourself did you lose connection with? Rediscovering those pieces is essential to building a fulfilling life post-divorce. This book offers not just inspiration but practical guidance on how to nurture yourself emotionally and physically, set meaningful goals, and regain control over your future.

This introduction sets the stage for the many layers of healing and growth that lie ahead. It's an invitation to be patient with yourself and to trust the process, even when the path isn't clear. You are not alone on this journey. Countless others have walked this road, emerged stronger, and found renewed purpose. Their stories of courage and perseverance illuminate the way.

Ultimately, this book isn't just about surviving divorce—it's about thriving afterward. It's about taking back your power, owning your story, and stepping into a future that's shaped by your values and dreams. Through the challenges and the breakthroughs, you'll discover that rebuilding your life after divorce can be one of the most transformative experiences of your life.

CHAPTER 1

The End Is Not the End

Divorce marks a profound turning point, but it's important to remember that it isn't where your story ends—it's the beginning of a new chapter filled with possibility. The storm of emotions that comes with parting ways can feel overwhelming: grief, anger, guilt, and even relief may swirl together, making it hard to see clearly. Yet, these feelings are all part of the healing process, and giving yourself permission to experience them fully is a crucial step toward reclaiming your sense of self. Divorce doesn't break you; rather, it challenges you to shed old identities and resist the shame or stigma that society often attaches to ending a marriage. Creating healthy emotional boundaries, especially when children are involved, helps carve out space for growth and peace. This period, while painful, holds the potential for transformation—where letting go becomes a powerful act of self-love that opens doors to hope and reinvention.

Facing the Storm of Divorce

Divorce feels like an unexpected storm that sweeps through your life, leaving everything rearranged, and often, much darker than before. The upheaval isn't just about changing your living situation or figuring out legal details—it's a total emotional tempest. Suddenly, long-held visions of the future no longer apply. The person you once thought would be by your side forever becomes a part of your past, and what was familiar turns strange and uncertain.

In these early days and weeks after separation, it's absolutely normal to feel overwhelmed. The storm makes it hard to see more than the immediate chaos. You might experience a whirlwind of emotions—anger, sadness, confusion, relief, guilt—all vying for attention, sometimes simultaneously. The intensity can be exhausting, leaving you drained in ways that don't always show on the outside.

It's important to acknowledge that facing divorce is much like weathering a natural disaster. You didn't choose the storm, but now you have to figure out how to protect yourself and rebuild what's left. This means learning to accept the pain without letting it define you. It also means holding onto hope, even when it feels nearly impossible to imagine feeling whole again.

Life after divorce often feels like stepping into uncharted territory. The safety net of your marriage has vanished, and with it goes the familiar rhythm of everyday life. You might question your self-worth or wonder how

12

your friends and family perceive you. These questions can feel overwhelmingly heavy, but they don't have to hold you hostage. The storm may test your resilience, but it will not break you if you let yourself harness both the pain and hope together.

One thing to keep in mind is that no two divorce journeys look alike. Some find themselves immediately motivated to make big changes; others might just seek to get through the day. Both are equally valid responses. The key is to go at your own pace. Allow yourself that grace; you don't have to rush healing or pretend you're okay before you truly are.

During this time, people often find themselves trapped between two worlds—the past that's firmly ended and the future that's barely begun. That line can feel like a confusing gray zone. You might miss the companionship of your former partner but also recognize the freedom that comes with new beginnings. These contradictory feelings are part of the storm's power, shifting quickly and unpredictably. It's okay to feel conflicting emotions. The storm isn't linear.

Feeling alone during this upheaval is common, even if friends and family surround you. Divorce can feel isolating because it touches on deep, personal wounds that aren't always easy to share. Sometimes, societal expectations or stigmas add layers of shame or embarrassment, making it tempting to hide your true feelings. But true strength lies in vulnerability. When you allow yourself to reach out—even in small ways—you're taking vital steps toward calmer skies.

Recognizing the emotional roller coaster is crucial. Some days you'll feel like you're rebuilding your life; others may find you stuck in sorrow or anger. This back-and-forth doesn't mean failure—it means you're human. Give yourself permission to experience every emotion without judgment, knowing that the storm will begin to pass in time.

This phase is also about reclaiming control where you can. Divorce often leaves people feeling disempowered. Finding even small areas of your life where you can make decisions for yourself—whether it's choosing how to decorate your new space, setting daily routines, or establishing new friendships—can offer a sense of stability amid the chaos. It's these moments that begin to lay the foundation for personal reinvention.

Planning too far ahead might feel impossible right now, and trying to force new goals can backfire. Instead, focus on short-term steps that nurture your well-being. This might mean prioritizing sleep, seeking support networks, or journaling your thoughts. Each small act of care is an anchor in the storm.

Facing the storm doesn't imply you have to go through it alone, either. Surrounding yourself with people who listen without judgment—whether it's friends, family, or professionals—can make the journey less terrifying. Sometimes just knowing you aren't the only one navigating these waters can bring unexpected relief.

It's worth remembering that the storm is unpredictable; there will be days that feel lighter and others dark with despair. Patience is essential—both with yourself and the process. Transformation rarely follows a straight path. Instead, it weaves through moments of hope and setbacks, grief and laughter, solitude and connection.

In some ways, this storm clears away what no longer serves you. It may reveal hidden strengths or passions that were overshadowed in the marriage. Though it's painful, the storm can ultimately awaken you to a freer, more authentic version of yourself—one that's capable of rebuilding with clarity and courage.

While the storm of divorce is undeniably fierce, it is not the end of your story. Far from it. Each gust of wind that threatens to knock you down also challenges you to stand taller. Every heavy downpour that darkens your path waters the seeds of growth waiting to emerge once the skies clear.

Facing the storm means accepting the full reality of your situation while refusing to be defeated by it. It's about feeling pain but refusing to be defined solely by it. Keep in mind that storms pass; sunrises follow the darkest nights. This moment in your life is a turning point—not a full stop—setting the stage for healing, rediscovery, and ultimately, renewal.

Understanding Grief and Loss After Separation

Grief after a separation often feels overwhelming and confusing. When a relationship ends, it's not just the loss of a partner—it's a loss of shared dreams, routines, and parts of your identity. The experience can be incredibly painful because it shakes the very foundation you built your life on. Many people underestimate how deep and multifaceted this grief can be. Unlike a single event with a clear timeline, the mourning process after divorce or separation tends to stretch out, unfolding in waves that catch you at unexpected moments.

It's crucial to recognize that grief doesn't follow a straight path or a schedule. Some days you might feel okay, and other days it hits hard like a tidal wave. This unpredictability is normal. Your emotions may swing between sadness, anger, relief, confusion, and nostalgia. You might find yourself reminiscing about good times while trying not to get stuck there. This back-and-forth pulls at your heart and makes it difficult to find a steady footing. It's okay to feel mixed emotions—that's part of healing.

Many people are surprised or frustrated by how long the grieving lasts. There's no magic number of weeks or months to wait before you're "over it." Sometimes the loss feels like it reopens at anniversaries, holidays, or unexpected triggers. This can feel discouraging, but it's actually a sign that your heart is still processing what happened. Each phase you move through chips away at the pain and slowly carves out space for new growth. Understanding this helps reduce the pressure to "move on" too quickly and allows you to grant yourself patience.

One of the toughest parts of this grief is dealing with the loss of future plans you once hoped for. When you and your partner envisioned a life together, you had a shared vision: milestones to reach, places to live, celebrations to enjoy. Separation abruptly cancels all that. It's natural to grieve those lost dreams just as much as the relationship itself. Your mind and heart will need space to mourn what might have been, even as you begin crafting what will be.

Grieving after separation also means mourning the changes in your daily life. The rituals and patterns you grew accustomed to—whether having coffee together, sharing weekend plans, or simply knowing someone was there—disappear. Loneliness can sneak in unexpectedly, even in the middle of a busy day. This everyday mourning can feel small but accumulates into a significant loss. Learning to recognize and honor these smaller grief moments helps in gaining control over the emotional tide rather than feeling swept away by it.

It's important to remember that grief affects people differently. Some express it openly through tears and talking, while others may internalize feeling emotionally numb or disconnected. Neither reaction is wrong. Our cultural tendency to associate strength with "keeping it together" may make it hard to share what you feel, but bottling up grief only delays healing. Finding a safe space—whether with friends, support groups, or a therapist—can help you work through your emotions authentically and without judgment.

Understanding the intersection between grief and identity loss can be enlightening. Many find that, during the marriage, their identity interwove closely with their role as a spouse. Once separated, it can feel like a part of yourself has disappeared. This creates a void that may cause confusion or lowered self-worth. Grief in this area isn't just missing someone; it's missing the version of yourself you knew before. Reclaiming that sense of self may feel daunting, but it's a vital step in moving forward.

Another hidden grief lies in the shifts within your social circles. Friends and family might take sides or drift away, leaving you feeling isolated not only from your former partner but also from your wider support network. This social loss compounds the main grief and can lead to feelings of loneliness or abandonment. Realizing that this is a normal dynamic prevents you from blaming yourself and encourages seeking new connections that can offer unconditional support during this time.

Grief after separation also isn't just emotional; it's physical, too. Stress shows up in many ways—exhaustion, changes in appetite, headaches, or trouble sleeping. You might not realize how much your body is carrying until you begin paying attention. Taking care of your physical health becomes an essential part of managing grief. Simple actions like daily walks, balanced meals, and consistent sleep routines aren't just good habits—they're powerful tools to stabilize emotional turmoil.

In many ways, grief is the price of love. When you invest so deeply in another person, losing that connection leaves an ache. The pain can feel unbearable at times, but it also proves your capacity to love profoundly. Holding onto this perspective can turn grief from something to fear into something to honor. By embracing the tenderness of your heart, you position yourself for genuine healing rather than avoidance.

There is no right way to grieve, no checklist to follow, and no timeline to adhere to. What matters is allowing yourself to feel all that comes up, even the messy, confusing, or contradictory emotions. Sometimes grief manifests as anger or frustration, which can actually be part of protecting yourself from further hurt. Naming these feelings without judgment creates a pathway to understanding rather than self-recrimination.

While it's important to feel your grief, it's equally crucial not to get trapped in the pain indefinitely. Grief evolves—it shifts from raw and overwhelming to something quieter and more manageable. This evolution opens room for acceptance and hope. You begin to see beyond the loss to the possibility of new beginnings. The end of a marriage isn't the end of your story.

Many people find that grief after separation eventually leads to profound personal growth. This transformation might come as a surprise, especially when pain feels so consuming at first. Yet over time, navigating your grief helps build resilience, self-awareness, and a stronger sense of independence. You uncover inner resources you didn't know you had before. This is where your journey truly begins—a journey from loss to rediscovery and empowerment.

The process of understanding your grief can be one of your greatest gifts post-divorce. By facing your feelings honestly, you honor the relationship you had and the life you envisioned. This honesty clears the way for forgiveness of yourself and your ex-partner, releasing bitterness or blame that only weigh you down. It's through this emotional clarity that you can finally start to reclaim your peace.

Lastly, giving yourself permission to grieve fully helps prevent what some call "complicated grief"—an extended state of emotional stuckness where healing doesn't progress. Instead of avoiding pain or rushing to "get over it," making space for grief encourages it to move through you. This active process means you're not passively hoping for the pain to fade; you're intentionally engaging with your emotions and guiding them toward resolution.

Understanding grief and loss after separation is tough but vital. It reminds us that while divorce closes one chapter, it opens the door to a new kind of life—one where you can rebuild, redefine, and rediscover your truest self. The storm of emotions may rage, but with each wave, you're one step closer to calm, growth, and eventual joy. The end is not the end—it's a powerful beginning.

When Love Turns into Letting Go

Letting go isn't easy. Especially when what you're releasing once felt like the center of your world. Divorce often means facing the heartbreaking reality that love, as you knew it, has changed or even ended. It's not just about the relationship dissolving but about the emotional journey that unfolds when love shifts into something quieter—a place where holding on no longer serves you. This transformation can feel like a loss of self, a loss of future plans, and sometimes, a loss of hope. But it can also be the beginning of something new, a chance to re-center your life on yourself.

What many don't realize is that loving someone and letting them go are not opposites. Instead, they often coexist. You can still care deeply, treasure the memories, and honor the good times while recognizing that holding on is preventing both you and your former partner from healing and growing. It's a painful release, but it's necessary. Letting go means stepping out of that painful loop where your heart wants what it can't have, and your mind knows you need to move forward.

The process of emotional detachment is rarely linear. On some days, you might feel like you're finally free, ready to embrace new opportunities and rediscover who you are. On others, sadness, anger, or confusion might overwhelm you, making it tempting to retreat into old patterns or regrets. Accepting this ebb and flow without judgment is a crucial part of letting go with grace. It's okay to have moments of weakness or doubt; healing doesn't demand perfection, just persistence.

Letting go also means changing the way you tell your story. Instead of defining yourself by what's lost, you begin to see your worth independently of that past relationship. You recognize that love was a chapter in your life but not the whole story. This shift is empowering. It opens the door to self-compassion and a new kind of love—the love you offer yourself. That foundation becomes the bedrock of the future you're building.

One of the hardest parts of letting go is saying goodbye to "what could have been." Maybe you imagined growing old together, shared dreams that will never come to life, or simply the comfort of having a partner beside you. Mourning those unrealized possibilities is part of healing. It's natural to feel grief for the dreams that have slipped away. This sorrow deserves space to be felt and honored because it embodies the love that once was.

In the midst of this emotional upheaval, it's important to remember that letting go is not about erasing the past or pretending things didn't matter. It's about accepting the reality of the present moment. It's about understanding that clinging to old pain or hoping for things to return to how they were only delays the healing your heart needs. Acceptance is often misunderstood as giving up, but in reality, it's a powerful act of courage and self-care.

You might find yourself wrestling with conflicting emotions. Maybe there's anger toward your ex, guilt about your role in the marriage ending, or sadness that the life you imagined is no longer possible. Standing with all that emotional weight is tough, but shadows can't exist without light. Recognizing and naming these feelings gives you control over them rather than being controlled by them. It's a fundamental part of reclaiming your own power.

Letting go also involves setting boundaries—not just with your ex, but with yourself. Giving yourself permission to disengage from destructive thought patterns or toxic interactions fosters emotional safety. When you stop ruminating on what went wrong or feeling responsible for things beyond your control, space opens for growth. Boundaries protect your healing journey and help you rebuild confidence in your own decisions and needs.

Sometimes, love turning into letting go feels like a betrayal of your own heart. How can you stop loving someone without feeling like you're abandoning a piece of yourself? This is where compassion becomes vital. You can acknowledge the love you had while recognizing that love should never keep you trapped in pain. Releasing someone out of love doesn't mean you didn't care; often, it's the most loving thing you can do for both of you.

As you move through this part of your journey, focus on what letting go allows you to gain: freedom from emotional entanglement, clarity about what you truly want, and room to rediscover joy on your own terms. This space creates opportunities for self-discovery and personal reinvention—the exact path toward rebuilding a life that feels authentic and fulfilling. Letting go becomes the turning point where you begin to act not out of desperation or heartache, but out of hope and determination.

It's also normal to fear the unknown. What will life look like without this person? Will you ever love again? These questions can loom large, but it helps to remember that your future isn't a repetition of the past—it's a blank canvas waiting for you. Each day you let go is one step closer to painting a picture you choose, filled with growth and new possibilities.

For many, this process is made easier by leaning on a support system—whether it's friends, family, or professionals who understand the complex emotions involved in divorce. You don't have to walk this path alone. Sharing your story, expressing your feelings, and seeking guidance are all parts of letting love turn into letting go. Expressing vulnerability can bring strength and remind you that healing is often a communal experience, not just an individual one.

In time, the sharp edges of heartbreak dull. Love that once felt like a chain loosens and eventually becomes a gentle memory. What remains is respect for the journey you took and admiration for the resilience you showed. Letting go doesn't mean you forgot—it means you chose yourself. And that choice, over and over again, leads to growth and peace.

Remember, letting go is a process—sometimes messy, sometimes slow, often surprising. But at its heart, it's a declaration that your life, your happiness, and your self-worth matter. It's the decision to step into your future with courage, knowing that love doesn't have to end in despair; sometimes, it simply turns into the freedom to begin again.

You Are Not Broken by Divorce

Divorce often feels like a seismic event shaking the very foundation of your life. The overwhelming emotions and the chaotic upheaval can leave you questioning your worth, your strength, and your future. But here's the truth that needs to sink in deeply: divorce does not break you. It may change your circumstances, alter your path, and challenge your beliefs, but it does not define your value or fracture your spirit beyond repair. You are whole, capable, and strong—even if it doesn't always feel that way.

When the marriage ends, it's easy to internalize the experience as personal failure. Many people blame themselves, thinking that if only they were different in some way, things might have turned out better. Those feelings are natural, given the intimate nature of relationships, but they're also misleading. Divorce is a complex process involving two people growing apart for many reasons—circumstances, values, communication breakdowns—not a reflection of your worth as a person. It's crucial to separate your identity from the status of your marriage. You have inherent value just as you are, regardless of the relationship's outcome.

It can feel tempting to categorize yourself as "broken," especially when the pain feels so sharp and the future seems uncertain. But "broken" implies something that needs fixing or something inherently flawed. In reality, divorce is more like a deep wound that, with care and time, will heal. And healing often leads to growth and transformation. This process can be messy and unpredictable, but it doesn't diminish who you are. In fact, many people discover parts of themselves they never knew existed during this time. You're not broken; you're evolving.

Recognizing that you're not broken is foundational because it sets the tone for your entire healing journey. When you begin with self-compassion and understanding, your perspective shifts. Instead of spending energy on self-judgment or guilt, you start to focus on rebuilding and rediscovering yourself. This shift is vital because it opens doors for positive change rather than keeping you stuck in despair or resentment. It's okay to feel lost, confused, or fragile. Those feelings don't mean you're less of a person—they mean you're human.

Most importantly, embracing this truth allows you to reject the stigma often associated with divorce. Too often, society paints a picture that divorce equals failure or shame. Many who face divorce live quietly with this misconception, hiding their pain from the world or burying feelings of inadequacy. But the reality is that divorce is a life event—not a life sentence. It doesn't erase your accomplishments, kindness, or the love you've shared with others. It's just one chapter closing so another can begin.

Consider the image of a tree battered by a storm. The branches may snap, leaves may fall, and the tree may appear damaged at first glance. But the roots remain deep and strong underground. Over time, new growth emerges from what was thought to be lost, even stronger and more resilient than before. You are like that tree. Divorce may feel like that storm, but your roots—your true self—remain intact and ready to support the new life waiting for you.

It's also important to understand that being "not broken" doesn't mean ignoring the pain or pretending everything is okay. Healing is messy. You will have moments of doubt, anger, sadness, and relief all mixed together. These emotions don't make you weak; they make you real. Allowing yourself to feel completely—even in the darkest moments—is part of maintaining your wholeness. Resilience isn't about avoiding hardship; it's about facing it head-on with courage and grace.

One way to reinforce the truth that you're not broken is by reminding yourself of your strengths and past victories. Reflect on times when you faced challenges—big or small—and found a way through them. Maybe you learned a new skill, rebuilt a friendship, or simply got up each day when it was tough to do so. These actions, no matter how seemingly insignificant, reveal your resilience and capacity for growth. Divorce may have changed your external circumstances, but it hasn't erased your inner strength.

Another vital piece is rejecting negative labels. Sometimes, after a divorce, people start referring to themselves as "failed," "unlovable," or "damaged." These words sting and can become self-fulfilling prophecies if allowed to take root. Instead, try shifting your language to something more empowering and nurturing. Say, "I am healing," "I am learning," or "I am enough." Language shapes how you see yourself and ultimately influences how you move forward.

You might hear others say, "You'll find love again" or "This is a fresh start," and while those statements hold truth, your journey of healing and self-acceptance isn't about rushing into what's next. It's about sitting with yourself firmly in the present moment, knowing that your value is not dependent on relationship status or external validation. This is your time to reconnect, nourish your soul, and build a foundation that's strong enough to support whatever life brings next.

Divorce can also bring unexpected gifts—hidden opportunities for self-discovery and reinvention. It invites you to explore parts of yourself that perhaps were dormant or overshadowed in your marriage. You might rediscover old passions, pursue new goals, or find independence previously unimagined. This process proves that you are far from broken; you are becoming more authentically you, free from constraints or expectations that once weighed you down.

It's natural to grieve what you lost—hopes, dreams, routines, and the vision you held for your life. Grief is not a sign of defeat but evidence of the depth of your investment in the relationship. Allowing yourself to mourn fully honors your experience and paves the way for healing. It's in this space, filled with vulnerability and honesty, that the belief "I am not broken" takes root most firmly. You accept the reality of your pain without letting it define your essence.

When it feels like the world is judging or pitying you, remember that your self-worth springs from within. No one else's opinion has the power to shatter your core unless you allow it. Your worth is not tied to your relationship status, your past mistakes, or what others think. It is inherent and unshakeable. Nurture this truth daily, especially when self-doubt creeps in. Write it down, say it aloud, put it where you'll see it—whatever it takes to remind yourself of your wholeness.

In this transitional time, be patient with yourself. Healing has no set timeline, and moments of weakness don't undo progress. There will be good days and difficult days, and both are equally valid and necessary. Recognizing your intrinsic wholeness doesn't mean you'll immediately feel okay—it means you accept that you deserve kindness and respect from yourself as much as from others.

Divorce may have changed the story, but it is not the end of yours. You are not broken; you are evolving, healing, and growing. Each day brings new chances to step more fully into who you really are. Let this section serve as a powerful reminder that the person you see in the mirror today is fundamentally whole and worthy of love—starting with the love you give yourself.

Debunking Divorce Shame and Stigma

Divorce often feels like stepping into a harsh spotlight, where judgment and misconceptions can swirl around you like a storm. For many, one of the heaviest burdens isn't just the end of the marriage itself—it's the shame and stigma that society can unfairly attach to divorce. But those societal whispers, those sideways glances, are rooted in outdated ideas that need to be called out and challenged. Divorce is not a failure, nor does it define the worth or character of the person going through it.

It's important to remember that the shame that some feel after divorce is often imposed externally, rather than stemming from the reality of the situation. What people don't often see are the complex emotions and efforts it takes to navigate a painful transition. They don't see the courage it takes to walk away from something that isn't working in pursuit of healthier, happier futures. Stigma around divorce can make people feel isolated or broken, but nothing could be further from the truth.

The shame around divorce often stems from societal expectations of marriage as a fixed ideal, something people are supposed to maintain at all costs. This black-and-white thinking ignores the messy realities of relationships, where love, growth, and compatibility evolve—and sometimes fade. When a marriage ends, it's not a mark of failure; it's a recognition that the partnership isn't supporting the growth or happiness that two people deserve. In fact, ending a marriage can require significant bravery and self-respect.

Many people also wrestle internally with blaming themselves, thinking they weren't "enough" or that their divorce somehow signals personal flaws. But self-blame can be a trap that pulls you deeper into pain instead of helping you heal. The truth is that relationships involve two people, and when they don't work out, it's rarely due to the failure of one alone. There are countless reasons marriages end, from growing apart to incompatible life goals or choices, and none of those are reasons to feel ashamed.

Stigma and shame can also have a gendered element. Women, in particular, often face harsher judgment in some circles, with stereotypes portraying divorced women as broken, bitter, or less desirable. Men aren't immune either, but society's expectations can differ. These stereotypes are unfair and inaccurate. They ignore the resilience, growth, and strength that come with starting over. Divorce can be a turning point, a chance to reclaim identity and live more authentically—something to be celebrated rather than whispered about behind closed doors.

Community and cultural norms play a huge role in fueling divorce stigma. In some communities, divorce may be seen as taboo, and people may even face exclusion or criticism for seeking a life beyond a troubled marriage. Those social pressures make it harder to vocalize your struggles and seek support. When silence prevails, shame grows unchecked. Breaking that silence becomes an important act—not just for oneself but for others who may be suffering in silence as well.

One of the most powerful ways to dismantle divorce shame is to talk openly about the realities of divorce. Sharing your story—even if it feels hard—can create connection and understanding. It reminds you that you're not alone and pushes back against the false narrative that divorce is a private shame. Of course, you don't owe everyone your personal history, but finding spaces where honest conversation is welcomed can be incredibly validating and healing.

Reflecting on the stigma attached to divorce can also reveal how much progress society has made—and how much further it needs to go. More people are now recognizing that divorce doesn't erase the years of love, commitment, or family built. It doesn't mean you're a failure or that your future is limited. Instead, more voices are stepping forward to tell stories of hope, resilience, and transformation after divorce. This cultural shift helps normalize divorce as a life transition rather than a scarlet letter.

Divorce shame is also closely tied to the myths about what a "good" life should look like. Some believe happiness only comes from traditional family structures, but that's simply not true. Life is complex, and happiness can come in many forms. After divorce, many discover new paths, friendships, passions, and forms of love that feel more aligned with who they really are. Rejecting the shame means embracing that freedom to define your own version of a fulfilling life.

For those navigating the aftermath, it's critical to recognize how harmful internalizing shame can be. It can sabotage self-esteem, increase anxiety, and keep you trapped in a cycle of self-criticism. Instead, practice reminding yourself that divorce is a chapter—not the whole story. You can honor the past while still moving forward with strength and hope. This shift in mindset can be a form of rebellion against stigma and a powerful step toward reclaiming your confidence.

Society's judgment can feel like an external voice trying to dictate your worth, but only you get to define who you are. Too often, shame silences the very real experiences of grief, loss, and growth that come with divorce. Giving yourself permission to feel without guilt or embarrassment is a radical act of self-love. As you do this, you chip away at the shame and create space for healing and reinvention.

One practical way to counteract stigma is to build or seek out supportive networks: friends, family members, or support groups that affirm your journey. Being surrounded by people who see your worth beyond your divorced status strengthens your resilience. Sharing experiences, advice, and encouragement helps replace shame with solidarity. It reminds you that many have navigated this path and found their footing again—often stronger than before.

Taking a step back, it's worth considering how cultural narratives about marriage and divorce evolve over time. In recent decades, divorce rates have shifted, and society's views continue to change as more people speak openly about their experiences. This trend is positive, but it doesn't erase the personal challenges of confronting stigma. Progress often comes one conversation at a time—from breaking the silence at family gatherings to advocating for realistic portrayals of divorce in media.

Viewing divorce through a lens of compassion rather than condemnation makes a big difference. Everyone's story is unique, and no one arrives at the decision lightly. The path to healing includes forgiving yourself for any mistakes, letting go of unrealistic expectations, and embracing the person you're becoming. It requires shedding shame, not layering it on further. When you reject stigma, you reclaim your voice and agency.

In the end, debunking divorce shame means shifting the story society tells about it. Divorce isn't an end to happiness or self-worth; it's often the beginning of rediscovery. Owning that truth helps you see that you're capable, strong, and deserving of a future filled with purpose and joy. When we confront stigma head on and refuse to let it define us, we create space for healing not only within ourselves but in the broader culture as well.

This new perspective—rooted in empathy and empowerment—is the foundation for rebuilding after divorce. It's an invitation to honor your journey, including the pain, and to find pride in your courage to start over. That transformation offers not just relief from shame, but a powerful blueprint for moving forward with dignity, confidence, and hope.

Permission to Feel Everything You're Feeling

When you're navigating life after divorce, one of the most difficult things to give yourself permission for is to feel everything that's swirling inside you without judgment or restriction. It's tempting to push away the raw emotions— anger, sadness, confusion, relief, or even moments of unexpected joy—because they can feel overwhelming or shameful. But here's a truth that often takes time to sink in: every feeling you're experiencing is valid, and allowing yourself to fully experience those feelings is a critical step toward healing.

Divorce isn't a clean break or a simple ending. It's a complex journey filled with loss on multiple levels—loss of a partner, plans you once had, stability, and sometimes even part of your identity. That complexity naturally stirs up an intense mix of emotions that don't fit neatly into categories like "good" or "bad." Sometimes you might feel numb, other times flooded. You might be surprised by anger or guilt you didn't expect. The emotional chaos isn't a sign of weakness or failure. It's part of being human.

Giving yourself permission to feel doesn't mean letting your emotions control you. It means recognizing their importance so you can begin to understand where they're coming from and what they're trying to tell you. Think of your feelings like waves in the ocean—some days they crash ferociously, other days they ebb quietly. Trying to hold back those waves or pretending they don't exist only causes more pain, but if you allow yourself to ride them, you'll find that the intensity eventually passes.

When feelings are dismissed or ignored, they tend to linger beneath the surface, sometimes manifesting as anxiety, depression, or physical symptoms. They can weigh heavily on your spirit, making it hard to move forward. By contrast, when you consciously acknowledge what you're feeling— without embarrassment, guilt, or criticism—you're laying the groundwork for emotional release. This process doesn't mean you have to live inside the pain forever, but you do have to make space for it at first.

It might be helpful to remind yourself that feeling deeply after divorce is not a sign that you're stuck. In fact, it's the opposite. It means you're fully engaging with your experience, honoring part of yourself that demands recognition. Allowing space for emotions like grief or anger doesn't prolong your journey, it enriches it. Over time, these feelings lose their power when they're met with acceptance rather than resistance.

Many people feel an invisible pressure to "be strong" or "get over it" quickly after divorce—what others often call resilience. But resilience doesn't mean you don't break down or cry. It means you let yourself break down, cry, and feel, and then you find the strength to keep going despite that. In fact, real strength grows from this emotional openness. You don't emerge from this chapter unchanged or numb; you come through with a deeper understanding of yourself and what you truly need moving forward.

Some emotions may come as surprises. You might feel guilt for hoping for a new beginning, or confusion when you're relieved despite the sadness. Maybe you're angry at your ex, or at yourself, or at the situation more broadly. These feelings can co-exist, sometimes jarring you with their contradictions. It's okay to have mixed emotions—it's part of the messiness of healing. The trick is giving yourself the grace to hold those feelings simultaneously without harsh self-judgment.

When you allow yourself to feel, it can also lead to moments of clarity. You might discover, beneath the surface sadness or rage, a core of hope or a longing you hadn't fully acknowledged. These insights are invaluable, because they guide your next steps—not as someone trying to forget the past or suppress pain, but as someone learning to integrate their experience into a renewed sense of self.

Creating this emotional permission can be challenging if you grew up in an environment where feelings were dismissed or seen as a sign of weakness. You might find yourself slipping back into old habits of self-criticism when emotions flare up. It's a common struggle, but one you can gently push against every day. Affirmations like "It's okay to feel this" or "My emotions are valid" can become small but powerful mantras that shift your mindset over time.

Allowing your feelings doesn't mean acting on every impulse they bring. Feeling anger, for example, doesn't mean you have to lash out. It means recognizing that anger exists and finding a way to express it constructively, whether that's through journaling, talking to a trusted friend, or channeling it into creative outlets or physical activity. Feeling your emotions fully is the first step. Knowing how to manage and express them comes next, and it's a skill you cultivate as you move toward healing.

Another important aspect is understanding that feeling isn't linear. There will be days where the pain feels fresh and acute, and others when there's a surprising sense of calm or even happiness. Don't pressure yourself to feel a certain way by a specific time. Healing after divorce doesn't come with a predictable timeline, and emotional ups and downs are part of the natural rhythm. Giving yourself permission to ride the emotional waves means honoring those rhythms without forcing progress.

In this permission lies a profound act of self-compassion. You're saying, "I see you. I see all of you." This kind of compassion is the foundation of rebuilding confidence and trust in yourself. When you stop rejecting or minimizing your feelings, you reclaim a crucial part of your inner power. You're no longer ashamed of your journey—you're embracing it as a vital step toward the life that awaits you.

Finally, remember that receiving support can help as you learn to permit your emotions fully. This may come from therapy, support groups, or close friends who don't rush you to feel better but simply listen and hold space for your feelings. You don't have to walk through this alone. Sharing your emotional experience out loud can often lessen the heaviness, turning the invisible burden into something shared and understood.

The end of your marriage is not the end of you. It's the beginning of a chapter that asks you to be brave enough to feel, brave enough to love yourself—and brave enough to move forward with a heart wide open to whatever comes next. Giving yourself the permission to feel everything you're feeling isn't just a step in the process; it is the process itself.

Cutting the Emotional Cord to Move On

Letting go after divorce isn't about forgetting what happened or pretending the pain never existed. Rather, it's about consciously choosing to detach the emotional ties that keep you stuck in the past. This process—cutting the emotional cord—can feel daunting, even impossible at times, especially when memories, regrets, and lingering feelings seem to cling tightly. But making that choice to emotionally untether yourself is one of the most powerful steps you can take toward reclaiming your life and moving forward.

It's important to understand that the emotional cord is invisible, but it's very real. It's that constant loop of thoughts that pull you back to moments of hurt, hope, or longing. It's the tug of unhealed wounds and uncertain futures. Without breaking free from this invisible tie, you risk living in a state of emotional limbo—neither fully here nor entirely free. The cord drains your energy, clouds your judgment, and keeps you imprisoned in what was instead of who you are becoming.

Cutting the cord doesn't mean you have to sever your humanity or crush every feeling that arises. That's impossible, and honestly, unhealthy. Instead, it's about accepting your emotions without letting them control you. Imagine holding your feelings in your hands like fragile, raw glass—acknowledging their weight and shape without dropping or smashing them. You give them their moment, then gently set them aside so they no longer dictate your every thought or decision. This creates space for new feelings to grow—hope, joy, and eventually, peace.

39

One of the biggest challenges is untangling your identity from the marriage that just ended. Many people tie their sense of self to the relationship—who they were as a spouse, the future they envisioned, the life they thought they'd have. When that relationship ends, those threads feel like they're unraveling your entire being. Cutting the emotional cord means beginning to see yourself apart from that identity. It's realizing you are whole and valuable on your own, independent of the past you shared. This shift isn't always immediate, but it starts with small, intentional steps of self-recognition and kindness.

Resentment and anger often act like knots along the cord, making it even harder to cut loose. Holding on to blame, wishing things had been different, or replaying conversations endlessly keeps you tethered to pain. While these feelings are natural, letting them dominate keeps the cord thick and strong. Forgiveness, whether of yourself or your ex, doesn't mean you condone harmful actions or forget lessons learned. Instead, forgiveness is the act of loosening those knots, allowing the cord to fray and eventually snap. This frees your heart from carrying unnecessary burdens and opens the door to healing.

It's also helpful to recognize the role that attachment plays in keeping this cord alive. Emotional attachments don't end just because a partnership does. They linger in routine, in familiar patterns, and in the rituals you once shared. Taking back control means disrupting these attachments—changing habits, creating new routines, and intentionally filling your life with experiences that affirm your individuality. Even small acts, like altering your daily schedule or redefining your living space, send a clear message to your brain: life is moving forward, and you're in charge of where it goes.

Some find it useful to visualize cutting this cord as a ceremonial act. You can write a letter that expresses everything you need to release—grievances, sadness, hopes, and fears—then burn or tear it up in a safe space. This symbolic gesture can help your mind mark a turning point. Others find meditation or focused breathing practices help untangle that emotional knot. The key is finding a method that resonates with you personally; the goal is to create a clear break, not a rushed escape.

Remember, cutting the emotional cord is not about rushing through your feelings or minimizing the significance of the relationship you had. It's about honoring that chapter of your life respectfully, then intentionally stepping away to make room for new chapters. It's possible to hold memories with gratitude even as you move on with purpose and clarity. This act of release can be deeply healing because it returns power to you. Instead of being pulled backward, you begin steering your own journey ahead.

There will be days when the cord feels tight again, when old feelings drift to the surface like waves pulling you in. That's normal. Healing isn't linear. Each time you acknowledge these waves without surrendering to them, the cord weakens a little more. Trust that persistence and patience with yourself will break these ties over time. This is not a sign of failure but a reminder that true emotional freedom is earned, not given.

Another crucial part of cutting the emotional cord involves setting boundaries—both internal and external. Sometimes, staying in frequent contact with an ex, or keeping oneself overly involved in their life through social media and mutual friends, acts like tying knots around the cord, making it harder to cut loose. Defining what is healthy for your mental space and respecting those limits makes the process smoother. This might mean muting social media updates, limiting conversations, or gently refusing to engage in topics that trigger old pain. Boundaries protect your progress and honor your healing journey.

In moments when guilt or second-guessing creeps in, remind yourself that cutting the cord is a self-respecting act, not a selfish one. It's the healthiest gift you can give both yourself and the people around you. When you are no longer emotionally drained or stuck in the past, you show up more fully, more authentically, and with clearer intention. The cord you cut isn't just about letting go; it's about gaining the freedom to love and live again on your own terms.

Practicing self-compassion is the glue that holds this process together. Instead of judging yourself for feeling "weak" or "unfinished," recognize that healing requires gentleness. If the cord doesn't come loose overnight, that's okay. Forgive yourself for any perceived missteps and celebrate small victories. Each moment where you reclaim your emotional energy is a triumph. Allow yourself to feel both the pain and the hope simultaneously because that complexity is real and human.

Ultimately, cutting the emotional cord is a gift you give yourself—an act of courage and resilience. It marks the beginning of a new phase where the past no longer controls you and the future becomes yours to design. You start walking with lighter steps and a stronger heart, ready to explore who you are beyond the relationship, embracing the person you're becoming. This freedom creates space for healing, happiness, and a renewed sense of purpose.

In this way, the end of your marriage truly doesn't have to be the end of your story. By cutting the emotional cord, you claim the narrative. You move forward with intention, empowered by your own strength, and ready to create a life filled with possibility. The past shapes you but no longer defines you, and that realization can open doors you never thought possible.

Navigating Guilt, Anger, and Regret Post-Divorce

Divorce stirs up a whirlwind of emotions, and among the most complex and persistent are guilt, anger, and regret. These feelings often sneak in unexpectedly, clouding your thoughts and stirring unrest. Recognizing that experiencing them is normal is the first step on the path to healing. You're not alone in feeling overwhelmed by these emotions, and it's important to give yourself permission to face them head-on rather than stuffing them away.

Guilt can manifest in many ways after divorce. You might find yourself replaying past mistakes or questioning every decision that led to the breakup. It's common to think, "Could I have done more?" or "Did I hurt my children or partner too much?" These thoughts, though painful, stem from a place of care and responsibility. But letting guilt fester only keeps you trapped in a cycle of self-blame. Instead, begin practicing self-compassion. Acknowledge that, like anyone, you did your best with the tools and understanding you had at the time. It's helpful to remember that relationships involve two people, and the ending rarely rests on the shoulders of just one.

Anger often bursts forth as a response to betrayal, disappointment, or the upheaval of your life's foundation. You might feel angry at your ex-partner, yourself, or the situation itself. This anger, while uncomfortable, serves a protective role. It signals that boundaries were crossed or that your expectations were shattered. Instead of judging yourself for feeling angry, try to channel that energy constructively. Exercise, creative expression, or even simply journaling about your anger can help you process it rather than allowing it to simmer beneath the surface and poison your outlook.

Regret is another common companion post-divorce. It might stem from wishing things had gone differently or mourning lost time and opportunities. Regret can be paralyzing if it dominates your thinking. The key lies in shifting your mindset: regret can become insight if you let it teach you without letting it define you. Every experience, even the painful ones, carries lessons that can strengthen your future. While you can't rewrite the past, you can choose how you move forward with the knowledge you've gained.

It's vital during this emotional storm to cultivate patience with yourself. Healing is neither linear nor quick, and you might find these feelings ebbing and flowing unexpectedly. Some days will be harder than others, and that's okay. Instead of forcing yourself to "just get over it," try acknowledging whatever you're feeling. Label the emotion, sit with it briefly, and then remind yourself it's temporary, and it does not dictate your entire story.

Family, friends, or support groups can play a crucial role in navigating these tough emotions. Opening up about your guilt, anger, or regret doesn't make you weak; it makes you human. Sometimes all it takes is another perspective to release some of the weight you carry. Just remember to surround yourself with empathetic listeners who validate your feelings rather than dismiss or minimize them.

One tool worth integrating during this stage is mindful reflection. When guilt or regret pull you backward, practice grounding yourself in the present moment. Focus on your breath, the sensations around you, and the reality you're living now—not the "what ifs" or "if onlys." Mindfulness helps create a buffer between you and your intense emotions, making them easier to observe without becoming overwhelmed. Over time, this creates space for new, healthier thought patterns to emerge.

Understanding the root of your anger can also be enlightening. Ask yourself what your anger is protecting or demanding. Are you angry because you feel powerless? Disrespected? Hurt beyond what's easily expressed? Answering these questions allows you to respond to anger not with suppression but with curiosity and care. When you treat your anger like a message to be decoded rather than an enemy to be vanquished, you gain insight into your deeper needs and boundaries.

Regret, especially, can trap you in a narrative that everything you lose is a failure. Yet, it's important to rewrite this story. Remind yourself that this ending carved out space for a new beginning. The decisions and changes that divorce brings aren't just losses—they're also openings to reclaiming your authentic self in ways that weren't possible before. The path forward is full of potential, and regret should never steal your right to imagine a life you love beyond the divorce.

While these emotions can feel isolating, they are part of a universal experience. Many individuals come out on the other side of divorce not just stronger but more self-aware and resilient. This isn't to downplay the hardship you're facing—it's huge, and it shakes your core—but it is also an opportunity for profound growth. Negative feelings won't disappear overnight, but by engaging with them honestly, you prevent them from dictating your future.

Practical steps can help you manage these difficult feelings day-to-day. Setting aside time to express what's inside through writing or conversations offers relief. Creating rituals that honor your journey—whether it's lighting a candle, taking a walk, or simply sitting quietly in reflection—can build a sense of control and peace. At times, professional support such as counseling or therapy can provide safe space to unpack guilt, anger, and regret with guidance.

Importantly, be gentle with your pace. Healing after divorce doesn't mean erasing your past or becoming someone else entirely. It means stepping into your own power with honesty about where you've been and where you want to go. Guilt, anger, and regret can feel like heavy burdens, but they don't have to weigh you down forever. They can be markers on your map—points of pain that've guided you toward deeper understanding and self-love.

Ultimately, learning to navigate these emotions equips you for a stronger, more fulfilled future. The end of your marriage isn't the end of your story. It's the start of a new chapter shaped by your courage to confront the hardest feelings and the wisdom you gain along the way. Embrace that journey with hope and trust that every step forward brings you closer to the life you deserve.

Creating Healthy Distance Even with Kids Involved

Establishing healthy boundaries after divorce is challenging enough, but when children are involved, it becomes a delicate balancing act. You want to protect your emotional well-being while still being present and supportive for your kids. The key is finding a way to create emotional and physical distance from your ex without sacrificing the nurturing environment your children need. This isn't about shutting the door completely or becoming distant as a parent. Instead, it's about building a new kind of relationship—one that's respectful, functional, and puts the kids' best interests first.

Boundaries after divorce are essential for healing. You might feel compelled to check in or engage constantly with your ex for the sake of your children's well-being. But you also need to protect yourself from falling back into old patterns of conflict or codependency. Creating healthy distance means learning to say no to unnecessary interactions that drain your energy, while still staying actively involved in parenting. This way, you're not sacrificing your emotional health or your kids' stability; you're actually strengthening your role as a calm and resilient parent.

One foundational step is to clearly define what kind of contact you'll have with your ex moving forward. This isn't about being cold or harsh—it's about setting limits that prevent old hurts from reopening. Agreeing on communication methods, times, and boundaries with your ex can reduce tension for everyone involved. For example, many newly divorced parents find it helpful to use text or email for scheduling and updates, which keeps conversations clear and less charged emotionally. Physical distance might mean sticking to your agreed-upon visitation schedules and avoiding dropping by unexpectedly. It's okay—and often necessary—to protect your space.

Kids are incredibly perceptive and often notice when their parents are tense or upset around each other. That tension doesn't just affect the adults; it influences the children's sense of security as well. When creating healthy distance, try to approach it in a way that models respect and calm for your kids. They need to see that even though their parents are no longer together, they can still get along enough to cooperate. This doesn't require being best friends—it requires professionalism and kindness. By modeling this behavior, you're giving your children a blueprint for handling tough situations maturely.

It's normal to feel conflicted during this transition. On one hand, you want to maintain a close family unit for the children's sake. On the other, you crave freedom from the emotional baggage your ex carries. Balancing these needs is the art of healthy distance. You don't need to be emotionally available to your ex in the same way anymore. Rather, focus on emotional availability to your kids. This means drawing a clear line between what you share and discuss with your ex and what remains private. Kids benefit most when the adults act like a united front on issues that affect them directly, without letting personal conflicts spill over.

Another important factor is protecting your mind and heart from endless conflict or manipulation. Some ex-partners might try to draw you into arguments or guilt trips disguised as co-parenting concerns. Recognize these traps for what they are. Healthy distance involves learning to disengage from toxic dynamics. You can calmly respond to necessary communication without getting pulled into old fights. This skill takes practice and sometimes outside support. Surround yourself with friends, counselors, or support groups who help you keep perspective and bolster your confidence in enforcing these boundaries.

Physical proximity during parenting time is inevitable, and it's natural to sometimes feel anxious or triggered in these moments. Preparing emotionally beforehand, and having strategies to stay centered, will help you avoid reactive behaviors that set the tone negatively for your kids. Deep breathing, focusing on the kids' needs, or having a set phrase ready to de-escalate tension can make a huge difference. Remember, your children watch your reactions closely. Showing them strength and calm under pressure teaches them resilience in their own lives.

Technology can be a double-edged sword in co-parenting. While communication apps designed for divorced parents can streamline schedules and reduce misunderstandings, constant notifications or messages can also make it feel like the boundaries are always blurred. Consider setting clear parameters for when you're available to respond. Parents often find it helpful to designate specific times to check in on messages rather than feeling "on call" 24/7. This reduces anxiety and helps maintain that crucial emotional distance—without neglecting your responsibilities.

Creating healthy distance doesn't mean you stop caring or being involved; it means you're protecting your energy enough to be the best parent possible. When adults are less consumed with conflict, the family environment becomes more stable and nurturing for children. This is where healing truly begins—not only for you but also for your kids. It's about redefining what family looks like now and showing your children that love and respect can survive change and challenge.

When emotions run high, sharing your feelings with trusted friends or therapists can provide the support you need without dragging the children into adult struggles. Kids don't need to be mediators or emotional supporters, so keeping their minds clear of parental tension is vital. Healthy distance helps safeguard those boundaries, ensuring your kids feel safe and loved, rather than caught in the middle.

Adapting to this new dynamic takes time, patience, and sometimes trial and error. You might find that what works one month needs adjustment the next as kids grow and schedules shift. Flexibility is important, but not at the cost of your well-being. Maintaining that line between cooperation and personal space is a commitment to yourself and to your children's emotional health. Over time, this approach creates a foundation where everyone can thrive on their own terms while staying connected in healthy, meaningful ways.

Ultimately, "healthy distance" is more than a boundary—it's a new mindset. It allows you to love fully and parent effectively without losing yourself in the process. With kids involved, this balance can feel fragile, but it's absolutely possible. As you navigate through the ups and downs, remember that setting and respecting these limits is a form of self-respect and courage. It empowers you to move forward with clarity, strength, and a heart open for healing.

CHAPTER 2

———⊃•✹•⊂———

HEALING FROM THE INSIDE OUT

Healing after divorce isn't about rushing to fix what feels broken, but instead about turning inward and nurturing the parts of yourself that have been neglected or hurt. It's a process that demands patience and kindness, a gentle peeling away of layers to finally reconnect with who you truly are beneath the pain and the chaos. This chapter is about recognizing the power you hold to rebuild your emotional foundation, starting with small acts of self-care and honest reflection. It's about learning to listen to your own needs, giving yourself permission to feel, and gradually releasing the weight of sorrow and anger that can hold you back. Healing from the inside out means creating a new relationship with yourself—one based on compassion, strength, and the unwavering belief that you deserve a life filled with peace and joy, no matter what your past holds.

Reclaiming Your Identity After Divorce

Divorce often feels like losing more than just a partner—it can feel like losing a part of yourself. When the partnership that shaped much of your life and decisions ends, the profound question arises: who am I now? This moment of reckoning can be unsettling but also opens the door to a transformative journey of rediscovery. Reclaiming your identity after divorce isn't about returning to who you were before marriage; it's about embracing a new, freer version of yourself, shaped by the experiences you've endured and the strength you've cultivated along the way.

The process starts with recognizing that your identity was never entirely defined by the marriage. Although a relationship can be a significant part of your life, it's only one chapter rather than the entire story. It's easy to fall into the trap of self-doubt or confusion during this period, wondering what makes you "you" without that role. The truth is, beneath the roles of spouse, homemaker, or partner, there's an individual with unique passions, values, and dreams that have maybe been waiting quietly for the right moment to shine again.

One of the most empowering steps in reclaiming your identity is peeling away the layers of doubt and societal expectations that may still cling to you. Divorce can bring with it a heavy burden of stigma and shame, especially for women, who society sometimes unfairly brands with labels that don't reflect their worth or complexity. Challenging these external voices and reminding yourself that your worth is intrinsic—not tied to your relationship status—is crucial. This mindset shifts you from feeling defined by an ending to recognizing your potential for fresh beginnings.

It helps to spend time alone, not as a form of isolation, but as a deliberate act of self-exploration. Solitude can be a powerful tool; it allows you to check in with what you truly value and believe without distraction. Maybe you'll uncover interests you had put aside or discover new passions that ignite your spirit. Reclaiming your identity is deeply personal, so listening to your own voice during this time matters more than anything else. Self-awareness becomes the foundation on which you can build a vibrant, authentic life that reflects your true self.

Divorce also forces a reevaluation of social circles and how you spend your time. People often find themselves gravitating toward those who support their healing and personal growth, while others might fade away. This natural pruning is part of reclaiming your identity—choosing connections that nourish rather than drain. Rebuilding your support system and surrounding yourself with positive influences can reinforce a newfound confidence and enable you to step into your new role with strength.

It's normal to feel uncertain or even lost during this identity reshaping. There's no perfect blueprint—no one-size-fits-all formula for who you're supposed to become. Instead, give yourself permission to experiment, to try new things, and to redefine what success and happiness look like on your terms. Maybe this means pursuing further education, rekindling long-forgotten hobbies, or taking career steps that were once out of reach. Each small choice helps paint a clearer picture of the person you want to be moving forward.

At the heart of this journey is self-compassion. Divorce can shake your confidence and make self-judgment easy, but being kind to yourself during this vulnerable stage speeds up healing. Accepting that you're human and that healing isn't linear frees you to move through setbacks without harsh criticism. Instead of aiming for perfection, focus on progress. Celebrate moments of courage, even if they seem small. These victories strengthen your sense of self and help you realize you're more resilient than you believed.

Reclaiming your identity often involves setting boundaries that protect your emotional space as you heal. This could mean limiting contact with your ex-partner, establishing clear priorities for your time, or saying no to obligations that don't align with your well-being. Boundaries act as invisible walls that safeguard your emerging identity, giving you room to breathe, reflect, and flourish. They're not about shutting others out but about creating a safe, supportive environment where you can thrive.

In addition, reframing your self-talk is a powerful technique to shift your inner narrative. Divorce can seed harmful beliefs like feeling unlovable or undeserving, but challenging these thoughts actively rewrites that story. Practice affirmations that reinforce your worth and purpose. Remind yourself daily that ending a marriage doesn't diminish your value—it's just a part of your life's evolution, not the definition of it. Small changes in how you speak to yourself can drastically impact your mindset and emotional state.

Another vital piece in reclaiming your identity is reconnecting with your body—allowing yourself to feel at home in it again. Divorce can be emotionally exhausting and take a toll on physical well-being, so engaging in activities that nurture your body helps restore a sense of balance. Movement, whether through walking, yoga, or dance, can reconnect you with your emotions and awaken vitality. Your body is a powerful anchor to the present moment, reminding you that life continues and that you have the agency to shape your story.

Spiritual or mindfulness practices can also offer grounding during this transitional period. Whether through meditation, journaling, or simply observing your thoughts with curiosity, these practices deepen self-awareness and reduce feelings of overwhelm. They cultivate patience and acceptance, two critical qualities when redefining who you are. Such moments of introspection help you tune into your authentic self, free from external pressures or past baggage.

Rebuilding your identity isn't about rushing into a new label or rushing to prove that you've "moved on." It's okay to pace yourself and to allow the process to unfold naturally. Each day brings an opportunity to learn more about who you are now and who you want to become. The freedom after divorce lies in the possibility to design your life aligned with your true feelings, desires, and strengths.

Ultimately, reclaiming your identity after divorce is about honoring your past without being chained to it. It's about recognizing that the end of a marriage can be the beginning of a profound transformation—a chance to develop into a wiser, more empowered version of yourself. This journey takes time, courage, and self-love, but it's one of the most rewarding paths you can embark on. You have the inner tools to heal, reinvent, and emerge stronger on the other side of this experience.

Remember, this is your moment to step into the fullness of who you are. Let go of the pressure to fit anyone else's expectations. Give yourself grace and space to grow. The identity you reclaim after divorce will be richer, more authentic, and filled with endless potential. It's not just about surviving this chapter; it's about thriving beyond it.

Who Are You Without the Marriage?

One of the most challenging questions you'll face after divorce is this: who are you now, without the marriage? When you've shared years, memories, and a life with someone else, it's easy to feel like your identity was intertwined with that relationship. Suddenly, that part of your story has closed, and it can feel like you're standing at the edge of a vast, unfamiliar space. The truth is, divorce doesn't erase your worth or who you are at your core. But finding and owning your individual self after the end of a marriage takes time, courage, and a conscious effort.

It's common to feel lost when the role you played within your marriage—partner, teammate, co-parent—is no longer part of your everyday life. You might catch yourself thinking in terms of "we" and "us," even when it's just "me" and "I" now. This shift can stir up confusion and sometimes even a fear that you're less whole or less valuable. Understanding that your identity isn't confined to your relationship is the first step to rebuilding your sense of self.

Divorce can strip away those familiar labels that once felt like a safety net. When those disappear, the raw truth stares back: who am I if I'm no longer carrying the title of spouse? For many, this question is more than just theoretical. It touches on everyday realities—your social circle, where you live, your routines, and how you see your future. All these pieces form your identity puzzle, and without the marriage there, it might feel like the pieces scattered beyond recognition. But here's the hopeful part: you get to gather those pieces back together in a new, authentic way.

One important thing to keep in mind is that your identity is not static, nor is it limited by one chapter in your life. Just like every experience before the marriage shaped who you became, your life after divorce can serve as fertile ground for new self-discovery. Think of this as a kind of rebirth—not because you're shedding your past, but because you're embracing who you were all along, alongside who you want to become. Your marriage was part of your journey, but it doesn't define your entire story.

Many people fall into the trap of defining themselves by their relationship status alone—as if that's the main thing that gives life meaning or value. That pressure can feel overwhelming. Society sometimes reinforces this idea, subtle and not so subtle alike, that fulfillment only comes from being in a couple. Letting go of that mindset is freeing. It creates space for you to explore your interests, dreams, and qualities beyond the lens of partnership. This isn't just about filling a void left by the marriage; it's about rediscovering the vastness of who you are.

You might ask yourself, "What parts of me did I silence or sacrifice because of my marriage?" It's easy to fall into this trap because the routine of a shared life often means adjusting or compromising parts of your individuality. Now is the time to give yourself permission to reconnect with those passions, talents, and desires you put on pause or pushed aside. Whether it's a hobby, a career goal, or a simple joy that felt lost over time, nurturing these elements helps restore your confidence and sense of self-worth.

Reasserting yourself starts with small but deliberate actions. Your mornings could include writing in a journal about what you want, think, and feel—without judgment. Pay attention to your reactions, likes, and dislikes as they emerge afresh. Your boundaries might have become blurred in the marriage, so clarifying what feels right or wrong now is essential for reclaiming your identity. This isn't always easy, especially if you've relied on your ex-partner's validation or shared decision-making. But learning to trust yourself again is key.

Sometimes the hardest part is the silence. Without the constant "we" conversations, the familiar roles, and the shared history around every corner, the quiet can feel overwhelming. It might wake up fears of loneliness or abandonment that have been lurking beneath the surface. But this silence can also be a powerful tool. It's the quiet space where your true self begins to surface, beyond external expectations or old roles. Allowing yourself to sit with that silence, to be with your own thoughts and feelings, gradually rebuilds your capacity for self-trust and inner peace.

Another powerful way to explore who you are outside the marriage is through the people and experiences you choose to engage with now. Your social world might change, and that's okay. Surrounding yourself with people who support and encourage your new journey makes embracing your identity easier. At times, you may need to let go of relationships that keep reinforcing an identity tied only to being someone's spouse. This realignment helps create room for connections that see you as your full self—independent, evolving, and strong.

It can also be helpful to think about your values and what matters most to you now. Sometimes, while inside a marriage, priorities become collective, and your own values take a back seat. Divorce offers the chance to reevaluate these foundations. What do you want your life to stand for moving forward? What principles do you want to live by? This clarity not only shapes who you are as a person but serves as a compass for your decisions and goals as you move into the next stage.

Many people discover that when they stop defining themselves by their marital status, they open the door to rediscovering their power and independence. Confidence builds when you realize that you can face life on your own terms. The self you feared was lost wasn't gone, just waiting patiently beneath the surface to be welcomed back. This awakening can be both humbling and exhilarating—an invitation to rebuild your life from the inside out.

Along the way, you might wrestle with self-doubt or old narratives that suggest you're incomplete or less valuable because the marriage ended. These internal critics don't tell the truth. You are whole simply by being who you are, divorced or not. Healing isn't about replacing the past or pretending nothing happened but about affirming your intrinsic worth beyond those chapters of your life.

This process will look different for everyone because no two journeys are exactly the same. Some find new purpose in creative outlets, work, or community involvement. Others reconnect with spirituality or spend more time cultivating self-love. Whatever your path, the common thread is this: You are enough on your own. The idea of "who you are" without the marriage is an invitation to meet yourself deeply and compassionately for the first time in a long while. It's an opportunity to live authentically, reshaped but unbroken.

In time, you'll look back and see that divorce was not an end but a new beginning. The "you" who existed before the marriage, the "you" within it, and the "you" after—all real and valid—combine to form a richer, more expansive version of yourself. Who you are without the marriage is not a blank slate but a canvas ready for the masterpiece you're about to create.

Embracing the Real You Again

Divorce often leaves you feeling like a stranger in your own skin. Who you were before, during, and after your marriage might feel like multiple versions of a person you barely recognize. The process of reconnecting with your authentic self can feel daunting, yet it's one of the most powerful steps you can take on your healing journey. Embracing the real you again means peeling back the layers of roles, expectations, and old narratives to rediscover the person beneath it all—the you who's ready to live boldly on your own terms.

At its core, embracing your true self is about reclaiming the identity that may have gotten lost amid the chaos of separation and heartbreak. It's common to feel as if your identity revolved entirely around your marriage, which can leave a vacuum once that part of your life ends. You might find yourself asking, "Who am I without that relationship?" That question isn't just natural; it's necessary. Allowing yourself to explore it without judgment creates space for growth and reinvention.

Remember, this isn't about rushing to redefine who you are based on what's expected of you or fitting into societal molds. Instead, this is your personal invitation to reflect on what truly matters to you now. Which parts of your personality have been dormant? Which passions and dreams have taken a backseat? Embracing the real you again means giving those pieces of yourself room to breathe and flourish.

It helps to acknowledge that identity is fluid, especially during major life transitions. The you of today might not be the same you that existed five years ago, or even last year. Divorce kickstarts a transformation that may feel unsettling but is full of potential. As you shed old attachments and beliefs, you naturally evolve toward a more genuine version of yourself. This process can be messy. Sometimes, it's filled with confusion and self-doubt. But take heart: discomfort often signals growth.

One practical way to begin this journey is by tuning in to your inner voice. The noise of divorce can drown out your own thoughts and feelings, making it difficult to hear what you genuinely want. Set aside moments each day—no matter how small—to check in with yourself. Ask questions like, "What do I need right now?" or "What activities make me feel alive?" Journaling can be helpful here, serving as a mirror for your evolving self-awareness.

It's also important to challenge the limiting beliefs that might have taken root. You might have absorbed messages suggesting you're "less than" because your marriage ended. Or perhaps you believe you have to be a certain way to be lovable or successful. These narratives do nothing but cage the real you. Identifying and questioning these negative thoughts is essential to reclaiming your freedom and cultivating self-compassion.

Surrounding yourself with supportive people who honor your authentic self can accelerate your healing. Sometimes, friends and family hold onto old versions of you, intentionally or not, which can hinder your growth. Seek out connections with individuals who encourage your new path and celebrate your courage to change. Their validation helps you trust your own worth and strengthens your resolve.

As you embrace who you truly are, you may notice a renewed confidence swelling inside. This confidence isn't about perfection or having all the answers. It's about the quiet assurance that you can face life's uncertainties because you know your core worth. It's what allows you to set boundaries, say no to what doesn't serve you, and carve out a life that feels fulfilling.

Integrating self-acceptance with this emerging self-confidence transforms your mindset. You stop resisting your emotions or denying uncomfortable parts of yourself. Instead, you greet them with kindness and curiosity. Healing from the inside out means honoring the full spectrum of your experience—the joys, the fears, the strengths, and the vulnerabilities. These all make up the real you.

One of the most healing acts is to reconnect with old interests or explore new ones that resonate with your current self. Your passions can be anchors that remind you who you are beyond titles like "ex-spouse" or "single parent." Maybe it's an art class you abandoned years ago or a hobby you've always wanted to try. Engaging in these activities can reignite your sense of joy and creativity, reshaping how you view yourself outside of your past relationship.

It's okay to take your time rediscovering yourself. Some days you'll feel clear and strong, other days uncertain and fragile. Both are a part of this journey. Patience, combined with consistent effort, pays off. The goal isn't to erase the past but to build a future where your true self feels seen, heard, and respected.

Remember that embracing the real you again is also about forgiveness—not just toward others but toward yourself. This means releasing blame, guilt, or shame associated with the end of your marriage. When you forgive, you create emotional space for self-love and authentic connection. Forgiveness doesn't erase what happened; it frees you to move forward without carrying emotional baggage.

When you embrace who you really are, you no longer seek validation through others' approval but from within. This shift empowers you to make life choices that genuinely reflect what you want, not what you think you should want. It changes how you show up in the world—more grounded, more aligned with your values, and more at peace with the past.

This renewal of self is a foundation for everything you'll build next. Whether you want to pursue new relationships, career opportunities, or simply deeper happiness, it all starts with honoring your real self. Each step toward embracing that person makes the post-divorce world less intimidating and more promising.

Healing from the inside out means giving yourself permission to be imperfectly whole. It's recognizing that the real you has always been there, sometimes hidden beneath layers of adaptation and survival. Now is the time to invite that person forward, to live out loud without apology or fear. The real you deserves to be embraced—and this chapter in your life will remind you just how powerful that truth is.

Self-Care as a Survival Strategy

When navigating the turbulent waters immediately following a divorce, self-care shifts from being a luxury to an absolute necessity. At this point, it becomes your lifeline—a grounding force amid the chaos of emotional upheaval. Divorce often unearths raw feelings, sudden loneliness, and an overwhelming sense of loss. Taking care of yourself isn't just about feeling better in the moment; it's about survival and laying the foundation for a new, stronger you.

Self-care, in this phase, often means tuning in to your deepest needs, which might be drastically different from what you expected before your marriage ended. It's about recognizing that your well-being isn't secondary to anything else right now—it's your priority. Whether it's carving out time for restful sleep, nourishing your body with wholesome food, or simply allowing yourself moments of breathing space, these acts serve as tiny but powerful rebellions against emotional exhaustion. They remind you that you deserve kindness, especially from yourself.

The rawness of divorce can make everything else in life feel harder than it normally would—simple daily tasks can become mountains to climb. That's why it's crucial to approach self-care not as a one-size-fits-all checklist, but as a fluid, evolving practice tailored to where you are emotionally and physically. Some days, it might look like meditation or journaling, while other days might call for something as simple as watching your favorite show unapologetically or going for a walk in the fresh air. Small acts accumulate, forming a buffer against the overwhelm.

One of the most important aspects of self-care during this survival phase is to give yourself permission to say no—to obligations, to emotional labor, and to anything that drains you unnecessarily. Divorce can leave you feeling stretched thin, pulled in all directions by legal matters, parenting logistics, social expectations, or even just the urge to prove you're "fine" when you're not. Recognizing where your limits lie and honoring them becomes an act of courage. It's about protecting your energy so you can heal.

Physical self-care plays a tremendous role in how you process emotional pain. You might not feel like hitting the gym or preparing elaborate meals, but even gentle movement like stretching or a slow walk can release tension trapped in your body. Nourishing meals don't need to be perfect or complicated; focusing on balanced, simple nutrition fuels your recovery. When your body feels cared for, it's easier to face the tough feelings head-on instead of burying them or letting them fester.

Emotional self-care, meanwhile, can be trickier. It means facing the pain and sadness without judgment but also recognizing when professional support might be needed. Therapy and support groups aren't signs of weakness—they're strategic tools that help you process and reframe what's happened. They give you space to unload the heavy load that no one else should carry for you. Moreover, leaning on trusted friends and family for emotional support is vital. Connection replenishes your emotional reserves, even if you feel like withdrawing.

In the chaos following divorce, self-care routines may be interrupted or feel impossible to maintain. But establishing even the smallest daily rituals—morning gratitude, a few minutes of mindful breathing, bedtime reading instead of scrolling the phone—can provide structure and predictability. This fosters a sense of safety in the midst of uncertainty. Remember, self-care doesn't have to be grand gestures; the consistency of small actions matters more than intensity.

Another critical component is learning to be patient with yourself. Healing isn't linear, and some days you'll move forward, while on others, the pain feels heavier than ever. Self-care as survival means accepting this fluctuation without harsh self-criticism. It's an acknowledgment that healing requires time, and kindness towards yourself creates fertile ground for growth. Each step you take, no matter how slow, is a victory.

Many who've traveled this path describe self-care as reclaiming their power when everything else feels out of control. It's about taking back choices that were often sidelined during marriage or the divorce process. When you pick what you'll eat, how you'll spend your time, or what boundaries you'll set, you reaffirm your autonomy. That empowerment acts like a shield, reducing feelings of helplessness and boosting confidence.

It's also important to shed any guilt tied to prioritizing yourself during this time. The narrative that placing your needs first is selfish needs to be challenged. In truth, pouring from an empty cup leaves you depleted and less able to engage with the people and responsibilities you care about. Self-care replenishes your capacity to love and show up authentically, not from a place of obligation or sacrifice but from abundance.

Self-care as a survival strategy is deeply connected to recognizing your value outside the confines of your former marriage. This transition period offers a unique opportunity to rediscover what makes you feel alive—whether that's a hobby, social connections, or simply quiet moments of reflection. When you nurture these parts of yourself, you remind yourself that you're whole and worthy just as you are.

It's worth noting that this survival phase of self-care doesn't happen in isolation. Sometimes, it requires a mindset shift from "fixing" or "getting over" things quickly to allowing space for healing at your own pace. The goal isn't to rush into the next chapter but to tend to your wounds thoughtfully so they transform into new strength. Think of self-care here as both shield and soil—protecting you now and nourishing the growth that's about to come.

In practice, this might mean setting intentional boundaries with people who don't honor your healing process or cutting down on social media and news consumption that triggers you. It can mean simplifying your environment to reduce stress or making time for creative outlets that allow you to process emotions indirectly. Every small choice contributes to building resilience and helps you transition from merely surviving to eventually thriving.

Remember, self-care isn't about perfection or checking off tasks from a list. It's about honoring your humanity and embracing your vulnerabilities. It invites you to listen to your body, mind, and heart, and respond with compassion. During this fragile phase after divorce, treating yourself gently is revolutionary and necessary. It plants the seeds for a future where you don't just exist—you flourish.

The journey through post-divorce pain is uniquely your own, and self-care as survival is your way forward through that darkness. Keep in mind that this practice evolves alongside you. What feels nurturing today might shift tomorrow, and that's okay. The key is commitment to yourself—steadily showing up even when it's hard, even when motivation flags. This consistent dedication to self-care creates a new foundation: a resilient self ready to embrace healing from the inside out.

From Barely Coping to Truly Thriving

After the whirlwind of emotions that divorce stirs up, it's easy to find yourself stuck in survival mode. You're just getting through each day, unsure if there's life beyond the exhaustion, sadness, or even anger you're feeling. Maybe you've lost track of who you really are behind the layers of pain and change. But moving from barely getting by—just coping—to actually thriving is not only possible, it's transformative. It's about shifting from a mindset of "just managing" to one that celebrates rediscovery, strength, and joy.

Healing isn't linear. You won't just wake up one morning and suddenly feel brand new. Instead, thriving after divorce often means embracing the days where you can only take small steps forward as much as the ones where you feel like you're soaring. A key part of that journey involves learning to trust yourself again—your decisions, your worth, and your path. The woman who once felt lost can become the woman who takes control of her life and defines success on her own terms.

It helps to remember that thriving doesn't mean being perfect or pretending everything's okay. Thriving means showing up for yourself, even when some days feel heavy.

It's a commitment to your well-being—not just physically, but mentally and emotionally too. This process includes recognizing your wins, no matter how small, and honoring the progress you make. Each moment you reclaim your power is a brick laid in rebuilding your foundation.

One of the biggest shifts from merely surviving to truly thriving is how you view challenges. Instead of seeing hardships as insurmountable barriers, you start to see them as opportunities for growth. Divorce forces you to face parts of yourself and your life that might have been neglected or hidden away. Once you begin to explore these areas with honesty and curiosity, you open doors to inner strength you didn't know you had.

It's common to feel disconnected from your sense of purpose in the early stages after divorce. Finding that purpose again can feel like a daunting task, but it often starts with little tastes of joy and interest. Maybe it's a new hobby, a chance to reconnect with old friends, or simply setting a daily intention to care for yourself. These small acts might seem insignificant at first, but they are the seeds from which your new, thriving life grows.

Thriving also depends heavily on creating a support system that truly sees you. For many women, divorce shakes the foundation of their social circles too. Some relationships might have shifted or faded, but out of that change comes the opportunity to build connections that uplift and empower you. The shift from isolation to meaningful community is crucial. Being around people who respect your journey and hold space for your healing can fuel your growth in profound ways.

Learning to nurture yourself deeply is another essential ingredient. While it sounds simple, self-care after divorce looks very different than the occasional bubble bath here and there. It's about prioritizing your needs consistently and compassionately. That could mean setting boundaries to protect your energy, seeking therapy or coaching to unpack complex emotions, or practicing mindfulness to anchor yourself in the present. These efforts pay dividends in resilience and clarity. Remember, thriving is as much about what you stop doing—like self-criticism or people-pleasing—as what you start.

Embracing your authentic self is at the heart of thriving. Divorce can strip away old identities—wife, partner, part of a couple—and leave you wondering who you are on your own. This moment, challenging as it is, also offers a blank slate. Here, you get to rediscover what makes you uniquely you, without compromise or limitation. Whether it's reinventing your style, pursuing new goals, or reconnecting with passions you once shelved, this exploration is vital. True thriving comes when you stop measuring yourself against past roles and start building the life you want based on your truest desires.

Financial independence often plays a big role in the transition from coping to thriving. Going through divorce can disrupt your financial footing, shaking confidence and stability. Taking charge of your money with clear plans and resources might feel intimidating, but it's an act of reclaiming power. Even small steps toward budgeting, saving, or learning about your financial options can boost your sense of control and brighten your outlook. It's empowering to know you're steering your own ship.

Alongside rebuilding external stability, managing internal habits makes a huge difference. Developing routines that support emotional healing and well-being anchors your growth. This doesn't mean rigid schedules or checklists, but rather, a flexible framework that fits your unique needs. Regular movement, nourishing meals, restful sleep, and mental breaks all contribute to a stronger foundation. When you care for your body and mind in tandem, your capacity to handle life's ups and downs expands dramatically.

Of course, setbacks are a natural part of the process and not a sign of failure. Some days you might feel like you're taking a step backward, and that's okay. Real healing honors patience and self-kindness. Thriving means embracing your humanity, with all its imperfections. Instead of pushing through with grit alone, it invites you to be gentle with yourself while staying committed to growth.

A powerful element of moving beyond coping is creating a vision of the future that excites you. After divorce, imagining what's next can feel overwhelming or even scary. But as you progress, the possibilities begin to come into clearer focus. This vision doesn't have to be life-changing overnight; sometimes it's simply allowing yourself to dream beyond survival. Setting goals that inspire you—whether personal, professional, or relational—can transform your

75

mindset from dragging through days to moving toward a horizon that feels worth waking up for.

In this phase, cultivating resilience becomes a daily practice rather than a rare achievement. Thriving is about bouncing back from difficulties while building inner strength that lasts. This strength comes from remembering your story—not just as a narrative of heartbreak, but as a testament to courage, adaptation, and renewal. You've faced challenges and made it through. Every step forward is proof of your capacity and will power.

Finally, the journey from barely coping to truly thriving invites you to claim your life as your own. It's about shedding any remaining feelings of shame, guilt, or self-doubt and standing tall in your newfound independence. You're not just surviving the aftermath of divorce—you're creating a vibrant new chapter filled with possibility and purpose. This is your moment to live boldly, love yourself fiercely, and redefine happiness by your own terms.

Building a Healing Routine That Works for You

After the upheaval of divorce, finding a way to rebuild yourself often feels overwhelming. Everything might seem out of place—your emotions, your daily rhythm, even your sense of who you are. That's why establishing a healing routine tailored specifically to your needs is crucial. It's tempting to reach for quick fixes or follow someone else's path, but the truth is that healing isn't one-size-fits-all. What works for one person might feel draining or stale for another. Your healing routine should reflect your unique story, your pace, and your emotional bandwidth at any given moment.

Building this kind of routine starts with intention. It's about choosing small, manageable actions that add up over time to restore your well-being and self-confidence. The best routines aren't about perfection—they're about consistency and kindness toward yourself. When life feels chaotic and unpredictable, having a set of reliable habits can anchor you. They create a safe space within your day, a moment where you can reconnect with yourself amid the chaos of change. But it's just as important to stay flexible and responsive to how you're feeling. Some days you'll need more rest; others, you might want to push yourself a little further.

Before jumping into crafting your daily healing plan, it helps to take a moment and assess where you are emotionally and physically. What feels most pressing right now? Are you drained and fragmented, needing gentle restoration, or are you ready to take on new activities that challenge your comfort zone? There's no shame in needing rest or wanting strength, and your routine can—and should—shift accordingly. It might change every few weeks as you progress or struggle, so be patient and give yourself grace to adjust rather than force adherence to a rigid plan.

One of the key elements in any healing routine is nurturing your body. Divorce often drags your energy down; it can disrupt sleep, appetite, and motivation. So, simple acts of physical care—like prioritizing hydration, getting outside for some fresh air, or even gentle stretching—lay a foundation for emotional healing as well. It doesn't require overhauling your entire lifestyle or following intense exercise regimes that leave you exhausted or frustrated. Instead, look for movement that feels good—whether it's a short walk in your neighborhood, a calm yoga session, or dancing in your living room to your favorite songs. These moments can boost your mood, release tension, and subtly remind your body it's still in your control.

Alongside physical care, mental and emotional habits deserve space in your routine. The divorce journey stirs up all kinds of feelings: confusion, sadness, anger, sometimes even relief coupled with guilt. Your routine should include intentional pauses where you allow yourself to tune into these emotions without judgment. Whether it's through journaling, meditation, or simply sitting quietly with your thoughts, these practices offer clarity and a steadying anchor for your mind. Over time, they help you observe your internal narrative and gently shift destructive patterns or negative self-talk.

Another essential practice to consider is connecting to uplifting, nourishing influences—people, experiences, or even media that soothe your spirit and remind you of your worth. Divorce can leave you feeling isolated even if you're surrounded by others. Including regular interactions with trusted friends, support groups, or a therapist can be a game changer. These connections provide a safe environment where your feelings matter and your story is heard without judgment. If in-person isn't possible or feels too exposing at first, online communities or even inspiring podcasts and books can fill that space and offer you a sense of belonging.

It's also important to build in moments of joy and creativity. Healing is serious, but it's not all heavy. A routine that balances emotional work with playful or fulfilling activities can spark hope and motivation to keep moving forward. This might mean carving out time for hobbies, exploring new interests, or simply indulging in things that light you up—even if it's just baking a favorite treat or watching a movie that makes you laugh. Inviting lightness into your life helps soften the weight of divorce and reminds you that happiness is not a distant dream.

While you're shaping your routine, be careful not to overload yourself. It's tempting to use productivity or self-improvement as a way to outrun pain. But pushing too hard can backfire, leading to burnout or deepening exhaustion. A good healing routine balances active self-care with restful recovery. Think of it as tending a garden: you plant seeds by showing up to your routines regularly, but you also allow space for the soil to breathe and absorb nutrients. Sometimes, the most healing act is simply pausing and being kind to yourself.

Many find it helpful to schedule their healing activities into the day—or at least map out roughly when and how they'll show up for themselves. Ritualizing these moments builds momentum and turns self-care from an occasional luxury into a regular habit. For example, beginning your day with a brief mindfulness exercise or ending it by writing a few lines in a journal can become a comforting rhythm. Over time, these small choices establish a sense of stability and routine amid the unpredictability of post-divorce life.

Remember, your healing routine doesn't have to be overly complicated or time-consuming. Even just ten minutes spent on something that nurtures your heart or mind counts as progress. The goal isn't to create a perfect checklist but to integrate practices that help you reclaim your inner strength and reconnect with who you are outside the relationship. In those moments, you're planting seeds of confidence and self-love that will grow steadily, even if the process sometimes feels slow or uneven.

Part of building a healing routine also involves recognizing and honoring your boundaries—both with yourself and others. Divorce can stretch you thin, especially if you're still involved with your ex, co-parenting, or navigating social circles that feel complicated. Protecting your emotional space means learning to say no without guilt, prioritizing your well-being, and resisting the urge to overextend in efforts to please others. Incorporate boundaries into your routine by setting aside dedicated time that's just for you—no interruptions, no obligations, just focused self-care. This intentional protection of your space reinforces your value and signals to yourself that your healing is a top priority.

Finally, expect your routine to evolve as you do. Healing isn't static, and neither should your self-care practices be. What feels right today might not tomorrow, and your changing emotions, energy levels, and life circumstances will all influence how you care for yourself. Embrace this natural ebb and flow by checking in regularly with yourself, tuning into what you need, and being willing to adjust your routine without judgment. Flexibility is a strength, not a weakness. It's how you stay connected to your inner wisdom and keep adapting your healing journey to what truly serves you.

Divorce is undeniably one of life's toughest challenges, but building a healing routine that works for you transforms the experience into an opportunity for growth and rediscovery. In creating this routine, you're not just surviving—you're giving yourself the tools to thrive again. Each deliberate step you take, no matter how small, is a testament to your resilience and your commitment to reclaiming joy, peace, and confidence in your life post-divorce.

Emotional Detox: Releasing Pain Gradually

Divorce shakes you to your core. The emotional upheaval can feel overwhelming—like you're trapped in a storm with no clear end in sight. But healing isn't about flipping a switch or rushing through the pain. It takes time, patience, and a gentle process of gradual release. This is where an emotional detox comes in: a step-by-step unburdening of the heart and mind to create a space where real healing can take root.

It's important to recognize your emotional detox as a personal journey rather than a quick fix. You won't wake up one day feeling 100% healed, but you'll notice shifts as you slowly unpack the weight you've been carrying. The pain you experience post-divorce isn't just something to endure—it's something to gently release, piece by piece, until it no longer controls your story. This gradual release makes way for hope, strength, and a renewed sense of self to emerge.

One of the hardest parts of this process is giving yourself permission to feel. Society often tells you to "move on" or "get over it" fast, but true healing respects the complexity of your emotions. Grief, anger, loneliness, regret—each feeling deserves recognition. Ignoring or suppressing them only prolongs your suffering. When you make space for these emotions, you become better equipped to understand their roots and work through them.

Start by observing your feelings without judgment. This practice can feel uncomfortable at first, but it's a vital part of the detox. When painful emotions arise, try to acknowledge them quietly and kindly, almost like meeting an old friend you haven't seen in a long time. Let yourself say, "I see you. I'm aware of you." This simple acknowledgment takes away some of the emotions' power to overwhelm you.

Letting go doesn't mean forgetting or losing respect for what you've been through; it means refusing pain's chokehold on your present. It's not a sudden erasure but a slow fading of intensity, much like how bruises heal over weeks. You might find that certain triggers—like anniversaries, places, or memories—still sting deeply. That's okay. Each encounter with those triggers presents another chance to process and release a bit more.

One way to aid this detox is to create a ritual or habit that encourages conscious emotional release. It might be setting aside a few quiet moments each day to breathe and scan your emotional state. You could create a safe space at home where expression feels non-threatening, perhaps with a journal, soothing music, or comforting scents. Rituals, even simple ones, give structure and intention to your healing efforts.

Writing about your feelings can serve as a powerful outlet. Pouring your heart onto paper removes some of the pressure building inside. You don't need to worry about grammar or coherence—just let words flow freely. Over time, you might notice recurring themes or questions. This awareness provides clarity and guides you on what to focus on next emotionally.

Therapy can also be a crucial tool in supporting your emotional detox. Engaging with a skilled therapist offers a safe and confidential container to unpack especially difficult feelings. It's a space where you won't be rushed or judged. Good therapy offers validation and teaches tools for self-compassion, resilience, and boundary building. Even if you feel hesitant at first, professional support often accelerates and deepens healing.

Self-compassion is the hidden key in this process. After divorce, it's easy to fall into the trap of blaming yourself or feeling unworthy of kindness. But healing demands you treat yourself as you would a wounded friend—with patience, forgiveness, and warmth. When negative self-talk creeps in, pause and challenge it. Ask yourself: "Would I say this to someone I love?" If not, replace it with gentler, more truthful messages.

Releasing emotional pain gradually also involves recognizing how physical habits influence your mental state. Stress and sadness often build physical tension—which in turn keeps your emotions stuck. Gentle movement—like walking, yoga, or stretching—helps liberate both your body and mind. Even deep breathing exercises can reduce anxiety and create a calm space to feel rather than fear your emotions.

Another vital aspect of emotional detox is peeling back layers of resentment and bitterness. These feelings can become heavy shackles that block you from moving forward. At first, these emotions may feel like protective armor. But when carried too long, they imprison you more than anyone else. Working through resentment doesn't imply forgetting or excusing hurtful actions; it means choosing your own freedom by lessening their emotional charge over you.

Patience is essential throughout this entire journey. Progress may look slow—and sometimes you'll feel like you've taken a step backward. That's entirely normal. Healing isn't linear. One day may feel like a breakthrough, another a setback. What matters is that you continue showing up for yourself consistently. Your willingness to face discomfort head-on is a courageous act of love toward your future self.

Perspective shifts slowly during this emotional detox. As the raw edge of pain dulls, you'll find space to see your experience from a new angle. Moments of clarity often emerge around when you least expect them—during a quiet walk, a conversation with a trusted friend, or even in your dreams. These insights are milestones on your path, signaling that your heart is adapting and growing.

Throughout this process, it helps to surround yourself with positivity—even if it feels small at first. This might mean reconnecting with supportive friends, listening to uplifting podcasts, or reading inspiring stories from others who have healed after divorce. This external reinforcement fortifies your internal commitment to letting go of pain and reclaiming joy.

Finally, remember that emotional detox isn't about becoming numb or emotionless. Instead, it's about freeing yourself from the constant heaviness of unresolved pain so you can fully experience all of life's colors again—even the joyful and hopeful ones. As you gradually release old wounds, you're creating the foundation for a stronger, wiser, and more authentic you to emerge.

Healing from the inside out means taking this detox at your own pace, honoring what you've been through, and allowing your heart the time and space it needs to mend. The journey ahead may be filled with ups and downs, but it holds the promise of renewal—a chance to shed the weight of yesterday and embrace the possibilities of tomorrow.

Clearing Out the Pain, Bit by Bit

Healing from a divorce isn't something that happens overnight. The pain, the heartbreak, the sense of loss — they all settle deep inside, and trying to erase them quickly can often make things worse. Instead, the process of clearing out the pain must be gentle, intentional, and gradual. Like peeling layers off an onion, bit by bit, you reveal your true self, finally freed from the heavy baggage of the past. This slow and steady unburdening is essential for lasting recovery and reclaiming your inner peace.

At the beginning of this phase, it's important to acknowledge that the pain doesn't simply vanish. It waits silently under the surface, and sometimes erupts when you least expect it—triggered by a song, a smell, or a passing thought. Understanding that these emotional waves are natural parts of the healing journey helps you approach them with patience rather than frustration. There's no timeline that fits everyone; each step you take, no matter how small, erodes the pain a little more.

Sometimes, the hardest part is sitting with your feelings without pushing them away. The instinct to avoid emotional discomfort can be overwhelming. However, suppressing or denying your pain prolongs its grip on you. Finding moments where you can quietly reflect—moments when you allow yourself to feel sadness, anger, or disappointment—marks the beginning of dismantling that hold. This doesn't mean wallowing endlessly but creating space for the pain to show itself, be witnessed, and then gradually loosen its grasp.

One practical way to clear out this pain is through establishing daily rituals that honor your emotional state. These aren't heavy or time-consuming tasks. They might be as simple as sitting with a cup of tea, going for a peaceful walk, or lighting a candle and setting an intention each morning. Over time, these small acts form a rhythm of care and gentle reflection that nurtures your healing. You start to reclaim control by choosing how to treat yourself during these vulnerable moments.

It's also key to recognize when old wounds resurface. Memories from the marriage, echoes of arguments, or reminders of what once was can bring a sudden sting. Instead of allowing these thoughts to spiral into self-doubt or despair, try to pause and observe them without judgment. Think of your mind as a garden that needs weeding: if you pick one hurtful thought and examine it, you can understand why it persists and then slowly uproot its power over you. This intentional mental work takes time, but it's liberating.

Clearing pain isn't only about confronting hurtful memories—it's about replacing them with new, healthier experiences. This might mean seeking out fresh activities, spending time with supportive friends, or rediscovering passions that slipped away during the marriage. These positive moments act like beams of light cutting through the shadows of grief. Even small bursts of joy remind you that happiness isn't permanently out of reach.

Another element of this process involves forgiving yourself where guilt or shame has set in. Many who've gone through divorce carry a heavy self-blame, replaying 'what if' scenarios endlessly. Gently unraveling these thoughts requires compassion. You're not imperfect because of what happened; you're human. Bit by bit, when you replace harsh self-criticism with kind acceptance, you chip away at the pain lodged deep within.

Social isolation often accompanies the heartbreak, which can magnify the pain. Reaching out—even with one trusted person—creates a vital bridge to healing. Sharing your story, voicing the ache, or simply spending time around people who understand can break the cycle of loneliness. Bit by bit, connection breeds hope and reinforces the belief that you aren't alone in weathering this storm.

It's worth emphasizing that this clearing process isn't linear. Some days, the pain may feel distant and manageable; other days, it may flood back stronger than before. That's normal. Healing curves, sometimes doubling back, but what matters is showing up for yourself consistently. Each small step forward, each moment of self-kindness, undermines the pain's power over time.

Mindfulness and grounding techniques also help here. When emotional waves hit, simple practices like focusing on your breath or feeling your feet firmly on the ground can prevent being swept away by overwhelming emotions. These tools let you regain presence—choosing calm over chaos, pause over reaction. Bit by bit, your nervous system learns new ways to respond, easing the intensity of past traumas and paving the way for peace.

Physical movement, too, plays a subtle but powerful role in clearing emotional pain. Exercise doesn't have to be strenuous; even gentle stretching, yoga, or walking can release stored tension in the body. Divorce often traps hurt in muscles and joints, and movement helps unblock stagnant energy. This process reconnects you with your body, an important aspect of reclaiming self-love and acceptance during heartbreak.

One important reminder during this clearing phase is to avoid rushing toward "fixing" everything. Healing is not a checklist or a quick fix—it's an ongoing journey. Allowing yourself grace to stumble, to rest, and to simply be is as crucial as actively doing the work. Bit by bit, you become that safe, understanding friend you needed most when things fell apart.

Lastly, consider the power of setting boundaries as part of clearing pain. Whether it's limiting contact with an ex-partner, cutting off negative social influences, or refusing to engage in conversations that reopen wounds, boundaries protect your fragile healing space. Every boundary you set is a statement: your wellbeing matters, and you're no longer letting past hurts dictate your emotional landscape.

Clearing out pain, piece by piece, reveals a surprising truth: even in the depths of loss, there is resilience. With each small act, you reclaim a measure of control, one bit of light returns, and your heart grows stronger. This phase isn't about forgetting the past but making peace with it—so you can finally open your life to what lies ahead.

Journaling, Therapy, and Self-Compassion Tools for Healing

After experiencing divorce, the internal landscape often feels like uncharted territory. You're not just navigating new routines or living arrangements—you're rediscovering who you are at your core. Healing from the inside out means engaging with your emotions deeply and authentically. This is where journaling, therapy, and cultivating self-compassion come into play. These tools help you process what you've been through, uncover patterns that might be blocking your growth, and nurture a gentler relationship with yourself as you heal.

Journaling isn't just about writing down the day's events or your to-do list. It's a powerful act of self-communication, a way to tap into your inner world when words spoken out loud might fail. Writing your thoughts and feelings down can help you catch and understand emotions that might otherwise swirl around silently. Sometimes, putting pen to paper reveals the underlying fears, doubts, or hopes you didn't realize were there. When faced with complex emotions like grief, anger, or loneliness, journaling acts as a safe container, keeping these feelings out of mental chaos and turning them into something tangible and manageable.

One of the reasons journaling works so well during post-divorce healing is that it allows for complete honesty without judgment. You don't have to worry about naming feelings "right" or explaining yourself to anyone else. This kind of freedom gives space for rawness to exist, which is a crucial ingredient in emotional healing. Over time, patterns will emerge as you revisit your entries—maybe moments when optimism peaked or days when despair crept strongest. Recognizing these ebbs and flows fosters curiosity rather than shame. It gives you insight into your own resilience and helps you plan for moments that challenge you the most.

Therapy can feel intimidating at first, especially if you're new to it, but it's a cornerstone resource for reclaiming your emotional wellbeing. Working with a trained therapist provides not just validation but guidance as you sort through the aftermath of divorce. Unlike journaling, where you're inside your own head, therapy gives you an external perspective—a supportive witness who can gently challenge negative beliefs or harmful thought patterns that might have taken root. Therapists also equip you with tools tailored to your unique experience, whether that's cognitive-behavioral techniques, mindfulness strategies, or trauma-informed approaches.

Importantly, therapy offers a confidential, neutral space to express feelings you might find difficult to share elsewhere. It becomes a place where you don't have to play a role or hide vulnerability. Many discover in therapy that grieving a relationship's end isn't a linear process; you might swing between relief, sadness, anger, or even hope. Understanding this rhythm can ease a lot of internal frustration because it normalizes what feels chaotic and overwhelming. When you start to recognize your own process, you'll feel more empowered to move through the pain rather than being stuck in it.

But therapy is just one part of the healing equation. Self-compassion also plays a critical role in transforming the way you relate to yourself post-divorce. All too often, people experience self-criticism that can be harsher than any external judgment. You might replay moments from the marriage or separation, blaming yourself for endings that are often complicated and multifaceted. Developing self-compassion means learning to treat yourself with the same kindness, patience, and understanding you would offer a close friend undergoing a tough time.

Incorporating self-compassion helps soften the inner dialogue that's often a blend of harshness and disappointment. It's about recognizing suffering without adding an extra layer of "should" or "if only." Instead of beating yourself up for feelings of loneliness or fear, you acknowledge them as natural human experiences. This shift, although subtle, has profound effects. It can lower anxiety, reduce harsh self-judgment, and build emotional stamina. Practicing self-compassion creates a foundation from which healing can genuinely begin, because it fosters acceptance instead of resistance.

There are many ways to cultivate self-compassion. Simple practices like mindful breathing or repeating affirmations can shift your mindset over time. You might also write compassion letters to yourself in your journal, responding gently to your inner critic. Another helpful approach is reflecting on how pain or mistakes have contributed to learning and growth rather than defining your worth. This reframing creates a narrative where you are more than your struggles—you are evolving, gaining wisdom, and worthy of care.

Pairing these tools—journaling, therapy, and self-compassion practices—can create a powerful synergy. Journaling maps your emotional terrain, therapy offers a reliable guide, and self-compassion provides the nourishing environment needed to embrace the journey. The act of engaging regularly with all three promotes self-awareness, supports emotional regulation, and strengthens your ability to face discomfort without recoil. This level of inner work allows you to shift from merely surviving the divorce to actively reclaiming your power and joy.

Healing isn't about rushing to "get over it" or erasing the past. It involves accepting that this chapter shaped you but doesn't define you. Journaling your thoughts becomes a testament to your endurance and evolution. Therapy becomes the certified ally who walks beside you when the path feels steep or uncertain. Self-compassion becomes the balm that soothes your wounds and encourages you to rise each day a little stronger. Together, these tools help rebuild your sense of self—one that isn't tethered to the end of your marriage but is expansive enough to hold your future dreams.

For those new to these practices, starting small is key. You don't need to write volumes every day or attend weekly sessions if that's overwhelming. Even five minutes of free-form journaling, a check-in with a therapist once a month, or a brief self-compassion meditation can make a difference over time. Consistency matters more than intensity. Over weeks and months, these intentional moments accumulate, gradually transforming your internal experience from one of fragmentation to wholeness.

It's also important to remember that healing tools are not one-size-fits-all. If a type of journaling doesn't resonate—say, morning pages or gratitude lists—try emotion-focused writing or letter-writing to the past self. If traditional talk therapy feels too rigid, explore art therapy or group sessions. If certain self-compassion exercises feel forced, experiment with body-based practices like yoga or gentle movement that cultivate kindness toward your physical self. What matters is finding what feels nurturing and doable for you personally.

Ultimately, the goal of journaling, therapy, and self-compassion exercises isn't to sidestep painful emotions but to build a stronger capacity to meet them without losing yourself. This process gradually empowers you to see that despite the hardship, you can emerge from divorce with a clearer sense of your values, needs, and hopes. You're crafting a new relationship with yourself—one rooted in understanding, acceptance, and the courage to rebuild. This inner work forms the heart of healing from the inside out, setting the stage for every step forward on your journey toward thriving, not just surviving.

CHAPTER 3

———— ⟩•✹•⟨ ————

REBUILDING YOUR LIFE WITH POWER AND PURPOSE

After the tumult of separation, it's crucial to reclaim control and start shaping your future with intention and strength. This chapter focuses on helping you envision a new life that feels authentic and exciting—one where your goals reflect your dreams, not your past constraints. Empowerment comes from setting clear, meaningful objectives and taking smart, steady steps toward emotional and financial independence. Confidence grows when you honor your decisions and embrace the freedom to redefine what fulfillment means to you. Whether or not parenting is part of your journey, this chapter guides you to stand firm, balance responsibilities, and nurture resilience every step of the way, transforming uncertainty into purposeful action.

Redesigning Your Vision for the Future

After the intense emotional upheaval of divorce, the idea of looking ahead can feel overwhelming or even scary. But redesigning your vision for the future isn't just about setting goals or planning what comes next—it's about reimagining your life on your own terms, with power and purpose guiding the way. You've been through a lot, and now the time has come to take stock of who you are now, what you want, and how to build a future that reflects your true self.

It's important to recognize that this transition period is not about rushing into a new version of life that simply fits what others expect from you. Instead, it's about peeling back the layers of doubt, fear, and hurt to discover what inspires you, what fills you up, and what makes you feel alive. You don't have to have it all figured out yet—that's part of the process. Redesigning your vision means opening yourself up to possibilities you might not have considered before and giving yourself the freedom to dream big without limits.

One major part of this redesign is shifting your mindset from scarcity to abundance. Divorce can leave you feeling drained, like resources—time, emotional energy, financial stability—are scarce and hard to regain. But the truth is, your future self doesn't have to be defined by what's lost. There's an abundance of opportunities waiting for you if you allow yourself to see them. This could be the chance to pursue passions you shelved for years or to finally invest in self-growth without hesitation. It's also about embracing the idea that your past does not dictate your future and that your worth extends far beyond the terms of your separation.

Another critical aspect is reconnecting with your core values and priorities. Divorce often upends a couple's shared goals, leaving individuals unsure where to anchor themselves. Now is the time to ask: What truly matters to me? What values do I want to guide my decisions and relationships moving forward? Whether it's honesty, creativity, kindness, or independence, knowing your values serves as a compass. When you align your future plans with what you deeply believe in, your vision becomes authentic and resilient, making it easier to stay committed when challenges arise.

Visualization can be a powerful tool here. Taking time to imagine your ideal life—without weighing it down by doubts or fears—raises hope and motivation. Picture your days, your relationships, your achievements. Allow your imagination to explore where you want to live, what kinds of people you want around, the energies you want to cultivate. This isn't about perfection but possibility. Those visions form the blueprint for your next steps.

It's also essential to recognize that redesigning your vision might involve redefining success itself. Traditional ideas of success—money, status, family—might not fit your evolving definition. And that's okay. Maybe success means cultivating deep friendships, nurturing your creativity, or prioritizing mental peace. Divorce often encourages us to throw out outdated scripts and write new ones that resonate with our present selves. This is your chance to decide what success looks like for you now.

As you craft this new vision, consider the importance of setting boundaries that protect your progress. It's tempting, and sometimes necessary, to say no to old patterns, toxic relationships, and habits that no longer serve you. Boundaries aren't walls; they're guardrails that keep your energy focused on growing toward what really matters. They help you create space for healthy connections and opportunities that power your transformation rather than drain it.

Remember too that redesigning your future isn't a solitary journey. It's okay to seek support—from friends, mentors, support groups, or professionals. Surround yourself with people who uplift you and align with your ambitions, who remind you of your strength when the doubts creep in. You deserve encouragement, and leaning on others is a sign of wisdom and courage, not weakness.

Financial independence plays a huge role in this vision too. Rebuilding stability after divorce can feel like climbing a steep hill, but envisioning financial freedom as part of your future empowers your decision-making. This may require relearning your relationship with money—budgeting, investing in yourself, and perhaps pursuing new career goals. Imagine a future where you control your finances and use them as tools to fuel your dreams, not tether you to old worries.

Alongside financial rebuilding, consider emotional independence as vital. You've lived a story that involved another person deeply, but your future depends on your ability to stand strong on your own. Emotional independence doesn't mean shutting down or isolating yourself; it means managing your feelings, finding your calm, and nurturing your resilience. It's about affirming that your happiness is not reliant on anyone else's approval or presence. This understanding creates a foundation for richer relationships and healthier choices down the line.

Divorce often forces an accelerated maturity in parts of life we didn't expect, and while that can be exhausting, it also plants seeds for incredible personal growth. Redesigning your vision is about honoring this growth while being gentle with yourself. You get to celebrate every small victory, whether that's learning to cook a new meal, returning to school, or finally letting go of bitterness. Each step is a thread weaving the fabric of your new story.

Now is your invitation to dream without limitation, to envision a future filled with meaning and possibility. Take the time to write down your thoughts, sketch your goals, and revisit your vision regularly as you evolve. Your journey after divorce is an opportunity not just to recover but to thrive, transform, and reinvent yourself with fierce intention. Your future is waiting—waiting to be shaped by your power, resilience, and purpose.

What Do You Want Now? Defining New Goals

After the whirlwind of divorce, you may feel like you're standing at a crossroads, unsure which path to take. It's a common experience. Once the dust settles, many find themselves wondering, "What do I want now?" This question isn't just about practical steps or immediate needs; it's about reconnecting with who you are and shaping a future that feels yours. Defining new goals after divorce is a powerful way to regain control, ignite hope, and step confidently into the next chapter of your life.

The first thing to understand is that your goals don't have to follow anyone else's blueprint. This is your life, and it's okay – more than okay – to forge a path that fits your unique circumstances, desires, and dreams. Divorce often forces a reset, but that reset offers an incredible opportunity. It's a blank page. You get to decide what success, happiness, and fulfillment mean for you now, not what they meant before.

One of the challenges many face is the pressure – whether internal or external – to have their new life all figured out immediately. It can feel overwhelming trying to map out all the details, especially while recovering emotionally. But defining your new goals doesn't happen overnight. It's a process that unfolds as you explore your newfound independence and rediscover your passions. This is a time for patience, curiosity, and openness to change.

Start by asking yourself questions that go beyond practical concerns. What lights you up these days? What have you always wanted to try but never had the chance to? What kind of person do you want to become? Allow yourself to dream without the weight of past limitations or fears. Setting meaningful goals is not about ticking off boxes; it's about creating a life that feels authentic and fulfilling.

It's also important to recognize that goals after divorce can take many shapes. They don't have to be huge, life-altering moves right away – though they can be if you're ready. Sometimes the smallest shifts, like committing to a morning walk, pouring time into a new hobby, or setting boundaries with toxic relationships, are powerful acts of rebuilding. These goals lay the foundation for bigger transformations. They help you build momentum one step at a time.

Defining your goals clearly helps your mind focus and reduces feelings of aimlessness. When you've been through divorce, it's easy to fall into auto-pilot, reacting to daily woes without direction. But as you articulate what you want, your choices start to align with those intentions. This alignment brings clarity and motivation, making it easier to take action, no matter how small, every day.

Consider breaking your goals into categories or time frames. For example, short-term goals might include things you want to achieve in weeks or months, like improving your physical health or reestablishing your social circle. Longer-term goals can stretch into years, like pursuing a career change, buying a home, or traveling solo. Breaking them down prevents overwhelm and keeps your vision manageable.

It also gives you more reasons to celebrate progress along the way.

Another part of defining new goals is recognizing that goals should reflect your current values and priorities. Your divorce may have drastically shifted what matters most to you. Maybe freedom, self-respect, and emotional stability now top your list. Or perhaps you're ready to pour energy into personal growth, creativity, or reconnecting with loved ones. Whatever feels most important, let those values guide your goal-setting. Doing so makes your goals feel relevant and deeply satisfying.

It's okay if some of your goals seem unconventional or unfamiliar. Maybe you decide to take a course in something you're passionate about, even if it's unrelated to your previous path. Or maybe you want to volunteer in your community or cultivate new friendships. These choices may surprise you, but they're part of the journey of rediscovery. Divorce can nudge you to open doors you never considered before, and that's a blessing disguised as a challenge.

As you define your goals, don't forget to check in with yourself honestly about what's realistic. Rebuilding your life isn't about rushing or forcing yourself into new roles just because you feel you should. It's about aligning your ambitions with your current mental, emotional, and physical state. That might mean pacing yourself, adjusting timelines, or seeking support from friends, mentors, or professionals. The key is to balance aspiration with kindness and flexibility.

Another element that's often overlooked is letting go of old expectations that no longer serve you. For example, you might have felt pressured to jump right back into dating or to prove to the world that you're "doing great." But your goals should come from your own desires, not outside pressures or comparisons. Defining what you want now means tuning out the noise and tuning into your own voice. That's how you build genuine confidence and inner strength.

Power comes from clarity, but purpose adds meaning. As you draft your list of goals, ask yourself how each one connects to your deeper sense of purpose. Purpose can be tied to your personal values, your passions, or even how you want to impact others. When your goals are purpose-driven, they become fuel for resilience. They keep you moving forward, especially on tough days, because they remind you why you started in the first place.

Goals don't have to be rigid or permanent. You have permission to revise, reinvent, or even abandon them as your journey unfolds. Life after divorce is unpredictable, and your vision for the future might evolve in ways you never expected. Staying open to change allows you to grow organically instead of feeling trapped by a plan that no longer fits. Remember, flexibility doesn't mean failure—it means you're learning and adapting.

It might help to write your goals down or create a visual representation, like a vision board. Seeing your aspirations clearly can reinforce your commitment and inspire daily action. Reflect on your goals regularly—weekly or monthly—

to assess your progress and adjust where needed. You might be surprised at how much your confidence grows just by recognizing small wins along the way.

Finally, defining new goals after divorce is an act of reclaiming your power. It's a declaration that your life is still full of potential and possibilities. With each goal you set and pursue, you build a stronger foundation of self-trust and self-respect. These qualities are crucial because they help you stand firm through setbacks and push forward with courage.

You don't have to know the whole picture right now. What matters most is that you decide what you want next and start moving toward it. This section of your journey is about discovering what truly matters to you, dreaming boldly, and taking those all-important first steps toward a future built on your own terms. The life you want is waiting – you just need to define it.

Letting Yourself Dream Again Freely

After the whirlwind of divorce, allowing yourself the space to dream again might feel both thrilling and terrifying. You've faced a profound ending, one that reshaped everything familiar, and now you're standing at a crossroads. It's completely natural to hesitate before imagining a future that feels uncharted. But dreaming freely is exactly what you need to begin rebuilding a life filled with power and purpose. This is your moment to rediscover what truly excites you, unbound from old expectations or fears.

What does it really mean to dream freely after a divorce? It's about more than just setting goals or making plans. It's the act of giving yourself permission to envision a life that reflects who you are right now, not who you were before or what anyone else expects you to be. Maybe you've spent years living within the confines of a shared marriage vision, or you put some dreams on hold to prioritize your relationship or family. Now, you get to choose what you want most—without apology.

New dreams may start small—perhaps the idea of traveling somewhere you've always wanted to go, picking up a hobby you abandoned, or exploring a passion you never had time for. Or, your dreams might grow into bigger ambitions, like switching careers, starting a business, or moving to a new city. Whatever form they take, each dream represents a declaration that your life is still full of possibility. You're stepping into an expansive space where hope replaces despair and action follows intention.

It's important to acknowledge that dreaming again doesn't erase the pain or the challenges you've faced. Those feelings might still linger and sometimes even try to convince you that you're not deserving or capable of happiness. But the act of dreaming is a powerful tool for healing. It reconnects you with your sense of agency and reignites your belief in the future. When you dream, you're practicing hope in its purest form, and that kind of hope can be a catalyst for transformation.

One way to let yourself dream without restriction is to silence the inner critic—the voice that says you're too old, too tired, or not enough. You might hear doubts rooted in past experiences or cultural messages that try to limit what's possible. Recognize those thoughts for what they are: fears, not facts. Give yourself the grace to explore what you want without judgment. Even if those dreams feel out of reach now, planting the seeds gives you a foundation to build on.

Visualizing your dreams can be a helpful exercise. Take time to imagine your ideal day, your ideal home, your ideal balance between work and play. What do you see? What feelings come up? These details matter because they anchor your aspirations in reality and make them feel tangible. Writing your dreams down or creating a vision board can also help you hold onto that hope and create a reminder to stay focused on what matters to you.

Another aspect worth highlighting is the freedom that comes with letting go of past limitations. Divorce can feel like the closing of a chapter, but it also signals the start of a new story—one where you get to be the author. This stage invites you to question old beliefs about what your life should look like and to break free from the "shoulds" and "have tos" that no longer serve you. Dreaming freely means opening yourself up to possibilities that might have seemed impossible before.

Sometimes, there's pressure—whether from family, friends, or even yourself—to quickly "move on" or conform to a certain path post-divorce. But rebuilding your life with power and purpose isn't about rushing. It's about thoughtful exploration. It's okay to take your time, to try out different ideas, and even to pivot as you learn more about what truly fulfills you. Freedom to dream encompasses the luxury of flexibility as well as courage.

Allowing yourself to dream also builds resilience. When you can picture a positive future, you gain motivation and strength to overcome setbacks that might come your way. Those dreams become a source of energy that pushes you forward, reminding you that your current circumstances don't define your destiny. Your imagination is, in many ways, a rehearsal for the life you're creating.

It's crucial to surround yourself with support that encourages your dreaming rather than stifling it. Seek out people who believe in your potential and respect your vision, whether that's friends, mentors, or support groups. Voices that lift you up help keep your courage alive, especially on days when doubt creeps in. Sharing your dreams aloud can give them weight and accountability, turning them into actionable intentions.

At the heart of letting yourself dream again freely is reclaiming your identity beyond the divorce. You're not just "the person who got divorced." You're an individual with hopes, desires, and the power to create meaning and joy anew. Dreaming is one of the first powerful steps toward rediscovery. It's your personal declaration that your best days are still ahead, and you're ready to pursue them actively.

Ultimately, the process of dreaming again is not just wishful thinking—it's an essential part of healing and growth. It invites curiosity, creativity, and vulnerability all at once. It reconnects you with your purpose because it demands you ask, "What do I truly want?" rather than "What's expected of me?" That question alone can shape a very different path forward, one rooted in authenticity and self-love.

Remember, your ability to dream is a gift—one that survived the storms you've endured. Nurture it, honor it, and protect it fiercely. Let your heart wander freely and don't be afraid to imagine a life that lights you up. This is your right, your freedom, and frankly, your next great adventure.

Financial and Emotional Independence After Divorce

One of the most transformative milestones in rebuilding your life after divorce is claiming both financial and emotional independence. These two aspects are deeply interconnected, yet each brings its own unique challenges and opportunities. When your marriage ends, it's not just the relationship that changes—your entire sense of security and self-reliance often shifts dramatically. But here's the truth: this moment marks the beginning of your ability to stand tall on your own, empowered by decisions that are truly yours.

Financial independence after divorce can seem overwhelming at first. Suddenly, you might be responsible for bills, savings, and daily expenses that were once shared. There's a lot to learn quickly—understanding budgets, managing debts, and planning for the future. This is about more than just dollars and cents; it's about rebuilding trust in your own ability to provide for yourself and, if applicable, your children without relying on a partner.

The freedom to control your finances is a crucial part of moving forward. It allows you to create a life aligned with your values and dreams instead of living within someone else's framework. Take the time to educate yourself—whether it's speaking with a financial advisor, attending workshops, or simply diving into budgeting tools and reading about money management. Remember, gaining financial confidence won't happen overnight, but every small step strengthens the foundation you're creating.

Simultaneously, emotional independence is just as important, though often more complex to navigate. Divorce can leave deep emotional wounds—feelings of loss, rejection, and uncertainty can linger. Separating your sense of worth from your marital status is essential. Your identity is not wrapped up in your marriage or its ending; it's rooted in who you are as a person, your strengths, your values, and your dreams.

Letting go emotionally means learning to thrive without needing validation or approval from your ex or anyone else connected to that chapter of your life. It's about building resilience so you can face the future with confidence instead of fear. Emotional independence is the freedom to enjoy your own company, to make decisions without second-guessing, and to nurture your well-being through self-compassion and clarity.

This emotional freedom also opens the door to healthier relationships down the road—whether that means friendships, family connections, or romantic partnerships. When you're stable emotionally, you set boundaries naturally and recognize what you truly deserve. You stop settling for less or falling into old patterns. Instead, you create space for authentic connections based on mutual respect and shared growth.

It's important to remember that rebuilding these forms of independence happens gradually and isn't a straight line. You may feel financially empowered one day and fragile the next. Some mornings you'll wake up feeling emotionally strong, while other times, waves of doubt or sadness will surface. These fluctuations are normal and a sign that you're healing. Instead of pushing these feelings away, honor them—they are part of the process that will ultimately lead to lasting self-reliance.

Another essential part of this journey is setting clear boundaries—not just with your ex, but with friends, family, and even yourself. Boundaries help protect your resources, time, and emotional energy so you can focus on what truly matters. Financially, this might mean being assertive about bill payments, savings, or financial support arrangements. Emotionally, it could involve cutting ties with toxic influences or saying no to commitments that drain you.

The empowerment that comes with financial and emotional independence also means learning to trust yourself again. Divorce often shakes confidence with so many "what ifs" and "should haves." But with time and intentional effort, you'll begin to hear your own voice clearly—your intuition, your preferences, your aspirations. Trusting yourself is the foundation for every decision you'll make moving forward, whether you're choosing a career path, pursuing education, or making lifestyle changes.

As your financial situation stabilizes and you gain emotional strength, don't overlook the power of celebrating your progress. Too often, the focus is on what's missing or what went wrong. Instead, acknowledge the victories—big and small. Paying a bill on time for the first time on your own, creating a new budget that works, setting a boundary that protects your peace. These benchmarks are proof of your resilience and growth.

One practical way to support your independence is to develop a mindset of abundance rather than scarcity. Divorce can leave many feeling like they're starting from zero, wondering if they'll ever recover. But abundance isn't just about money—it's about believing there's enough opportunity, love, and happiness ahead. Cultivate gratitude for what you do have, no matter how small, and visualize the life you want to build. This kind of outlook invites creativity and solutions instead of fear and limitation.

Another tool in your arsenal is cultivating a solid support network that encourages your independence rather than undermines it. Seek out friends, mentors, or support groups that empower you to make independent choices without judgement or unsolicited advice. Surround yourself with those who celebrate your progress and help you stay accountable without controlling your path.

Financial and emotional freedom also means embracing self-discipline and patience. There will be times when old habits or fears tempt you to revert to dependence or passivity. Fighting these urges requires commitment to your new life and the vision you've set. Remember, independence doesn't mean doing everything perfectly—it means persisting even when it's hard and learning from setbacks.

Ultimately, achieving independence after divorce equips you with more than just survival skills. It restores your sense of power and possibility. You'll find yourself dreaming again, not from a place of fear or limitation, but from a place of hope and courage. When you manage your resources thoughtfully and honor your emotional health, you create a life that's authentically yours, filled with strength, purpose, and freedom.

This chapter isn't about rushing into independence or trying to "fix" everything immediately. It's about recognizing what you deserve—a future shaped by your own hands. Embrace the process with kindness toward yourself. Financial and emotional independence after divorce is possible, and when you fully step into it, you'll unlock a life richer than you might have imagined.

Smart Steps to Rebuild Stability in Your Life

After the upheaval of divorce, regaining a sense of stability feels both urgent and elusive. The familiar ground you once stood on has shifted beneath your feet, and chaos can easily seem like the new normal. But stability isn't about erasing all uncertainty; it's about creating a foundation you can rely on as you move forward. Think of it as building a strong home from the inside out, brick by brick. It's a process that requires intention, patience, and self-awareness. And the good news is—you're fully capable of putting these smart steps in place, even if it doesn't feel that way just yet.

One of the first moves to create stability is setting clear, manageable routines. When life's whirlwind has thrown everything off balance, predictable rhythms can serve as anchors. This doesn't mean packing your days with endless tasks, but rather building small rituals that bring a sense of order. It could be as simple as morning stretches, a regular mealtime, or a nightly wind-down with a book. These small acts might seem minor, but they accumulate into a reassuring pattern. Over time, these routines help train your brain to expect calm and consistency—things that your heart desperately needs after so much upheaval.

Financial stability is another crucial pillar that can't be overlooked. Divorce often brings monetary uncertainty, which can amplify feelings of stress and fear. Taking control here means facing finances head-on, rather than avoiding them. Begin by getting a clear picture of your current financial situation—income, expenses, debts, and assets.

From there, create a realistic budget that prioritizes essentials and gradually rebuilds your savings. If you feel overwhelmed, don't hesitate to seek advice from a financial counselor or look for trustworthy resources online. Having a plan, no matter how small the steps initially, cuts through financial chaos and offers real peace of mind.

Beyond the practical, stability also means protecting and nurturing your emotional wellbeing. Divorce shakes your emotional foundation, and you may find yourself swinging between hope and despair. At this stage, cultivating healthy emotional boundaries becomes a form of self-preservation. This could mean choosing carefully who you share your feelings with, limiting contact with people who trigger doubt or negativity, or simply carving out time for yourself without distractions. When you honor your need for emotional space, you create a peaceful inner environment which is essential for clear thinking and gradual healing.

It's also wise to identify and focus on what you can control during this uncertain time. It's easy to get stuck obsessing over what went wrong or what could've been different. While reflecting can be part of healing, it shouldn't consume you. Instead, shift your energy toward actionable steps—like rebuilding friendships, setting goals for your career, or exploring new hobbies. These forward-moving actions create a sense of momentum and prove to yourself that you're still capable of growth, no matter where you've been.

Support systems are another critical piece of the puzzle. Stability doesn't mean going it alone. Surround yourself with people who uplift you—friends, family, support groups, or even professionals such as therapists or coaches. Having consistent, reliable connections that understand where you're coming from provides emotional ballast. They offer perspective, encouragement, and sometimes just a listening ear when things get tough. Importantly, these relationships should have boundaries that allow you to feel safe and respected. When support is steady, your foundation for moving on grows stronger.

Physical health is often overlooked but intimately tied to overall stability. The stress of divorce can take a significant toll on your body, sometimes without you even realizing it. Prioritizing sleep, nutrition, and some form of movement—even if it's just a daily walk—lays the groundwork for resilience. When you feel physically drained, emotional recovery slows down. By taking care of your body, you're fueling your ability to handle challenges and make clear, confident decisions.

Another important strategy is learning to manage your expectations, both of yourself and the process. Healing and rebuilding don't happen overnight. There will be days that feel like two steps forward and one step back. That's normal. Giving yourself permission to move at your own pace reduces pressure and allows for genuine progress. Celebrate small victories, whether it's sticking to your budget for a week, getting enough rest, or simply waking up with a more hopeful outlook. Recognizing those wins builds your confidence and wires your brain for hope instead of despair.

Rebuilding stability also means cultivating adaptability. Life after divorce is rarely linear; surprises will come, plans will change, and setbacks might feel discouraging. Flexibility lets you bend rather than break when unexpected challenges arise. This could mean adjusting your goals, revisiting your routines, or even redefining what stability looks like for you as you grow. When you welcome change instead of resisting it, you find strength in the very uncertainty that once felt paralyzing.

Setting goals that are both meaningful and achievable is a powerful way to regain control and create a sense of direction. Smart goal-setting means being specific about what you want and breaking it down into manageable steps. Start small—focus on short-term goals that feed into a bigger vision for your life. Maybe it's finishing a certification course, saving enough for an emergency fund, or carving out time to reconnect with your passions. Each goal you set and achieve is a building block for your new life's foundation, showing you that you're moving forward with intention and grace.

It's important, too, to cultivate a mindset that embraces self-compassion. Divorce often leaves you wrestling with guilt, regret, or self-blame. Stability thrives when you treat yourself like you would a close friend—with kindness and understanding rather than harsh judgment. Being gentle with yourself reduces inner turmoil and helps build emotional stamina for what lies ahead. Regularly remind yourself that this journey is about progress, not perfection, and that falling down doesn't mean failure—it simply means you're human.

Finally, as you take these smart steps to rebuild stability, keep reminding yourself that you aren't defined by your past or your divorce. Stability carries a lot more power when it's linked to purpose. When daily acts of rebuilding become part of a larger vision for your life, even the toughest days feel meaningful. You're laying the groundwork not just for security, but for a life filled with confidence and new possibilities. Remember, this phase is your chance to redesign your world on your own terms—with power, purpose, and a clear sense of who you are becoming.

Confidence in Your Own Decisions Moving Forward

After the upheaval of divorce, it's natural to feel uncertain about your choices. When the foundation of your life shifts, every decision can seem loaded with pressure and doubt. But confidence in moving forward isn't something that magically appears overnight—it's rebuilt step by step, like laying bricks for a new foundation you can trust. It starts with understanding that your ability to make good decisions remains intact, even if it's been buried under layers of pain and confusion.

One of the biggest challenges post-divorce is learning to trust yourself again. You might second-guess everything from daily tasks to major life moves because the voice inside you—one that used to feel reliable—may have grown quiet or shaky. The key is remembering that confidence isn't about never making mistakes; it's about embracing your ability to learn and adapt as you go. Every choice you make is an opportunity to build that trust, piece by piece. It's okay if you don't get it perfect the first time. What matters is that you keep showing up for yourself.

The path to confidence often starts small. Simple decisions create momentum, whether it's picking a new hobby, volunteering, rearranging your living space, or setting boundaries. These seemingly minor acts of choosing for yourself reaffirm your autonomy—and with autonomy comes power. Over time, those everyday choices accumulate, reinforcing your sense that you can steer your own life. This steady build-up eventually leads to embracing bigger decisions with less hesitation.

It's important to address the ghost of doubt that often follows divorce. Self-doubt can creep in disguised as worry about judgment from others or fear of failure. It might tell you that you're not qualified to make financial decisions, that you should follow others' advice to stay safe, or that your feelings don't count enough to shape your future. Recognizing these voices for what they are—internal critics without the final say—helps strip them of some of their power. When you catch yourself thinking, *"I can't do this on my own,"* pause and counter with a reminder of past challenges you have overcome. You've survived this painful chapter, and that is proof of resilience.

Another vital part of developing confidence is giving yourself permission to define your own path, free from external expectations. Society often places a heavy burden on how "success" should look after divorce—remarriage, financial stability, or social reintegration. While these can be goals, they don't have to be your only benchmarks. Confidence emerges when you set goals that resonate deeply with your values and desires, not just what looks good to others. Trusting your inner compass rather than following a prescribed map is a revolutionary act of reclaiming your life.

In learning to trust yourself, it helps to recognize that seeking advice or support doesn't undermine your decisions—it can empower them. Mentors, friends, therapists, or coaches provide perspectives that help you clarify your thinking. But remember, the final choice belongs to you. Feeling confident means owning that responsibility fully, without deferring to others out of fear or insecurity. It's a balance of humility and assertiveness, knowing when to listen and when to stand firm in your own truth.

Sometimes confidence takes a hit because of past hurts or mistakes. The self-critical stories we tell ourselves about what went wrong in the marriage or in the choices leading up to the divorce can weigh heavily. To rebuild confidence, it's essential to practice self-compassion—treating yourself with the same kindness and understanding you'd offer a close friend. Forgiving yourself for decisions that didn't turn out well is crucial. Every experience, good or bad, contributes to your growth and wisdom. Without this acceptance, it's hard to move forward because you're constantly anchored by regret and self-judgment.

When you find yourself overwhelmed by major decisions, breaking them down into manageable steps can prevent paralysis. Instead of trying to tackle everything at once, prioritize what matters most and create actionable plans. Whether it's choosing a new career path or figuring out living arrangements, taking your time—and breaking down the process into smaller bites—builds confidence in chunks. This method also allows space for reflection and adjustment, which is essential when starting fresh.

Developing confidence in your decisions also means leaning into your strengths and acknowledging what you bring to the table. Divorce can sometimes damage your self-esteem, but it doesn't erase your skills, experiences, or core character. Reflect on moments in your life when you've shown courage, resilience, and grit—these qualities are just as much a part of your decision-making toolkit as logic or planning. When you expand your definition of what makes a "good" decision to include emotional intelligence and intuition, you open the door to making choices that truly fit your authentic self.

A helpful exercise is to journal or verbalize your thought process when facing a decision. Writing down your options, fears, goals, and potential outcomes provides clarity. It also externalizes your internal dialogue, making it easier to challenge negative or irrational thoughts. Over time, this practice can reveal patterns in your thinking that either support your confidence or hold it back. You can then work on nurturing the positive habits and gently correcting the anxious or doubting ones.

Remember, confidence is not about knowing every answer in advance. It's about being willing to take risks, fail, reassess, and try again without losing faith in yourself. Each experience, no matter the outcome, sharpens your ability to make sound decisions. Confidence grows in this cycle of action and reflection—a constant process rather than a fixed destination.

Building confidence also means being able to embrace uncertainty. Divorce often shatters the illusion of control many people once had over their lives. Trusting your decisions in this new unpredictable landscape can feel like stepping into the unknown. Yet it's precisely in this space that your true resilience and inner power shine the brightest. Viewing uncertainty as an opportunity—not a threat—shifts your mindset from fear to possibility. This shift transforms how you approach decisions, turning them into moments of creative potential.

Finally, surround yourself with environments and people who reinforce your sense of worth and capability. Confidence isn't developed in isolation. Healthy social connections encourage your growth and affirm your evolving identity. Avoid those who feed doubt, shame, or negativity. Instead, choose relationships that inspire and challenge you in positive ways. Your circle can dramatically influence how confident you feel when navigating new chapters of your life.

As you move forward, keep celebrating every decision you make, no matter how big or small. Confidence is a muscle; like any muscle, it grows stronger with use. When you push through discomfort and choose yourself, you reinforce the truth that you are capable, worthy, and deserving of the life you want to create. This confidence doesn't just guide your decisions—it transforms your entire experience of post-divorce life into a journey filled with power and purpose.

Parenting After Divorce (If Applicable)

Navigating parenting after divorce means stepping into a role that blends strength with sensitivity, recognizing that your children need stability even when everything around them feels uncertain. It's about finding balance—maintaining your own emotional well-being while showing up consistently for your kids, supporting their healing without losing sight of your own growth. Setting clear boundaries and communicating with your co-parent in a way that prioritizes the children's best interests can reduce conflict and make the transition smoother for everyone. Remember, being a resilient and loving parent now doesn't mean you have to do it perfectly; it means being present, adapting as you go, and modeling courage through change. This phase offers a chance to redefine family dynamics on your terms, grounded in respect and hope rather than past pain.

Staying Strong for Your Kids Through Transition

Navigating life after divorce brings its own hardships, but doing so while supporting your children is a uniquely challenging journey. The emotional turmoil and upheaval don't just affect you—they reverberate deeply within your kids' lives, shaping their worldviews and emotional well-being. Staying strong for them doesn't mean suppressing your own feelings or pretending everything is perfect; rather, it's about fostering resilience through authenticity and steady presence.

Children often absorb the tension, uncertainty, and sadness in ways adults don't always notice. This makes it essential to act as a consistent anchor amid the waves of change. Stability might look different now than before, but finding routines and rituals that provide predictability offers a foundation your kids can rely on. Whether it's a nightly dinner, a weekend tradition, or simply your regular, genuine check-ins, these moments convey safety and signal that, despite the shifts happening around them, your love and commitment remain unwavering.

Understanding your kids' unique responses to the divorce also helps you meet their needs more effectively. Some children may respond with anger or withdrawal, others might cling tightly or become overly independent. Recognize that these reactions are their ways of processing the painful reality. Staying strong means cultivating patience and empathy, even when their behaviors challenge your own emotional reserves. It's okay to acknowledge that parenting through this transition is tough—it is—and showing your vulnerability at appropriate moments can, in fact, deepen trust and connection.

As you rebuild your own life, carving out space for your healing is vital—not just for you, but for your kids too. Children pick up on your emotional energy, so investing in your mental wellbeing isn't selfish; it's necessary. When you foster your own strength and clarity, you're better equipped to respond thoughtfully rather than react out of stress or fatigue. Simple self-care routines, therapy, or support groups can replenish your capacity, allowing you to be more present and patient with your children's ups and downs.

Communication remains key throughout this process. Encourage your kids to express their feelings without fear of judgment or dismissal. Let them know their emotions—whether sadness, confusion, or frustration—are valid. Sometimes silence or small gestures feel safer for children than talking, so be gentle and willing to meet them where they are. Open channels don't have to be formal or long conversations; short, honest moments can build bridges of understanding and shared strength.

Another aspect of staying strong is setting healthy boundaries, both for yourself and your children. Your new life dynamics may require redefining roles and expectations clearly. Kids need to know there are boundaries held by a steady hand, which provide safety and respect, but these cannot be rigid walls. Flexibility grounded in consistency allows everyone to adapt while still feeling secure. Your role evolves as the family system changes, and part of staying strong is embracing that evolution without guilt or doubt.

It's also important to shield your children from adult conflicts, especially those involving your ex-spouse. Being the calm in their storm doesn't mean staying silent about the divorce, but rather filtering what you share and how you discuss your former partner. Kids will pick up on tension and animosity if it's openly shown, which can lead to divided loyalties and confusion. Displaying respect and civility models emotional maturity and teaches your children how to navigate difficult relationships constructively.

Of course, staying strong does not require perfection. There will be days when you feel overwhelmed, frustrated, or unsure. On those days, it's okay to admit you don't have all the answers. Children often learn best by watching how adults handle imperfections—acknowledging your struggles and showing commitment to growth can empower them more than a facade of unbreakable strength. This balance between honesty and support creates a nurturing environment where resilience thrives.

As you face the inevitable moments of sadness or setbacks, remember that your example becomes a roadmap for your children on handling adversity with grace and fortitude. This transition period is a real opportunity to teach life skills that will serve them long after the dust settles from divorce. Lessons on coping, flexibility, empathy, and self-respect imparted through your actions can shape their emotional intelligence and self-confidence.

In sustaining your kids through this upheaval, be mindful too of the small victories. Celebrate moments of laughter, shared joy, and progress, no matter how modest they seem. These are powerful reminders that life after divorce doesn't have to be defined by loss alone—it can also be a season of growth, deeper connection, and new beginnings for your family. Your strength, even when quietly steady or imperfect, becomes the cornerstone of that hopeful foundation.

The path ahead is neither linear nor without its challenges, but staying strong through this transition means embracing the reality of your situation with compassion—for yourself and your children. It means showing up, day after day, with the intention to heal together, while empowering your kids to find their own voices and resilience. This shared journey of rebuilding is a profound demonstration of love that will sustain all of you far beyond the immediate aftermath of divorce.

Co-Parenting Without Losing Your Mind— navigating the complexities of co-parenting after divorce can feel like walking a tightrope stretched taut over a chasm of frustration, hurt, and exhaustion. It's a challenging adjustment, especially when emotions still run high and boundaries are being redefined. But it's important to remember: you're not alone, and it's possible to find a way through that balances your well-being with your children's needs. The goal isn't perfection; it's survival with grace, and gradually building a new rhythm that works for everyone involved.

First, let's get one thing clear: co-parenting is its own kind of partnership. It's not about rekindling a relationship with your ex or pretending that everything is okay. It's about creating a functional, respectful dynamic that prioritizes your children's stability. That means setting firm emotional boundaries and keeping communication focused on practical concerns. It's okay—even necessary—to cut through drama and avoid falling back into old patterns that served you neither during nor after the marriage.

One of the biggest hurdles is managing communication. It's tempting to vent feelings or send passive-aggressive messages, but doing so only adds fuel to the fire and complicates the co-parenting process. Using clear, direct, and neutral language can save a lot of headaches. Think of your conversations like emails to a colleague: stay polite, clear, and focused on the topic at hand—the kids. Avoid rehashing the past or bringing in unrelated grievances. This kind of communication might feel unnatural at first, especially when emotional wounds are still fresh, but it helps keep things smooth and predictable, which ultimately benefits everyone.

Technology can be a huge help here. Apps designed specifically for co-parents allow you to share calendars, schedule visits, and exchange messages in one place without the risk of misunderstandings through texts or calls. Using these tools takes the guesswork out of coordination and reduces unnecessary contact. Plus, having a written record can protect you if disputes arise down the road. Take the time to explore what tools might work best for your situation. Streamlining communication shouldn't be underestimated— it's a key stress-reducer.

Another cornerstone of co-parenting without losing your mind is managing expectations—not just your ex's, but your own. Accept that you won't control every detail, and sometimes things will go sideways. Kids get sick, schedules change, and emotions run high on all sides. Flexibility becomes a superpower here. Holding on too tightly to how "things should be" breeds disappointment and tension. Instead, cultivate an attitude of problem-solving rather than blame. When conflicts arise, step back and ask, "What's best for the kids right now?" Let your compassion guide you more than your frustration or anger.

Of course, putting your children first doesn't mean sacrificing your own mental health or peace of mind. Without your own strong foundation, you can't effectively support your kids. That means prioritizing your self-care and creating clear boundaries to protect your emotional energy. For example, set limits on when and how you communicate with your ex. If conversations become hostile or overwhelming, it's okay to pause and return to the discussion once things have cooled down. Learning to say no without guilt is crucial. Remember, you model healthy boundaries for your kids by practicing them yourself.

Consistent routines are vital for children during this chaotic time. Kids thrive on predictability, which anchors them amidst change. Working with your ex to establish routines around school, homework, bedtime, and holidays—even if imperfect—gives your children a sense of security. Sometimes, this means negotiating compromises, but it's worth the effort because it stabilizes their world. When each household respects similar rules and schedules, kids can transition more smoothly between homes. Stability is a gift, no matter what challenges you face in co-parenting.

You may find yourself tempted to involve your children in conflicts or use them as messengers, but protecting them from adult disputes should be your top priority. Children don't need to be confidants or peacemakers. Keep conversations about divorce and disagreements off their shoulders. They should never feel like they have to take sides or fix things between you and your ex. Encouraging open communication between you and your children separate from co-parenting conflicts reassures them that both parents love them unconditionally. This emotional safety net helps them adjust and heal.

When co-parenting gets especially tough, support networks make all the difference. Lean on trusted friends, family, or support groups who understand what you're going through without judgment. Sometimes, talking to others who've walked the same path offers fresh perspectives and practical tips. Professional counseling, whether individually or family therapy, can also be a wise investment to help you process feelings and develop coping strategies. Healing yourself empowers you to be the calm, steady force your children need.

It's also important to acknowledge that your relationship with your ex will likely evolve over time. What feels impossible now might become manageable years from now as wounds heal and new patterns settle in. Patience can be hard when tensions run high, but small steps toward respectful interaction build a foundation for long-term co-parenting success. Celebrate small victories, like a peaceful exchange or meaningful collaboration on a school event—they're proof progress is possible.

Being intentional about your mindset has enormous power. Viewing co-parenting as a form of teamwork centered on your children's well-being helps reframe what might feel like a never-ending battlefield. This shift doesn't erase pain or disagreement, but it channels focus toward a shared goal. You're both parents, even if no longer partners. Choosing to act with kindness and respect preserves your dignity and models resilience for your children. Over time, this intentional approach reduces stress and creates a healthier environment for everyone.

Remember, you are allowed to seek peace in this challenging chapter. Between juggling schedules, plenty of emotions, and your own healing, co-parenting may seem like an uphill climb. Yet, every small step forward builds momentum. Developing patience, boundaries, and clear communication set the stage for a co-parenting relationship that protects your sanity and nurtures your children's well-being. You're not just surviving this—you're rebuilding stronger, wiser, and more compassionate than before.

CHAPTER 4

———— ⊂•✳•⊃ ————

REWRITING YOUR STORY

After weathering the upheaval of divorce and beginning to rebuild, it's time to take the pen firmly into your own hands and rewrite the story of your life on your terms. This chapter is about embracing the truth that your past doesn't have to define your future, and that every ending carries the seed of a new beginning. It's a call to open your heart to fresh possibilities, whether that means rediscovering love, finding forgiveness, or simply reclaiming your peace and purpose. Remember, this is your comeback story—one where resilience transforms pain into strength, bitterness fades into freedom, and you emerge not just as a survivor but as the author crafting a vibrant new narrative of hope, confidence, and empowerment.

Love After Loss: Opening Your Heart Again

Emerging from the storm of divorce often feels like stepping out into a world that's both familiar and entirely new. After the intense experience of loss, the idea of opening your heart again can seem overwhelming or even impossible. Yet, healing doesn't just mean moving on—it means making space for love, in whatever form that may take now. This section is about reclaiming the courage to let your heart be vulnerable once more.

It's normal to carry scars from your past relationship. Those wounds shape how you view love moving forward. But healing allows you to rewrite the narrative, to build new patterns from the ashes of what once was. Opening your heart doesn't mean forgetting or erasing the pain you endured; it means giving yourself permission to experience connection again, without being held captive by fear or bitterness.

One of the first steps to opening your heart after loss is to acknowledge your feelings honestly. Grief, anger, confusion, relief—they're all part of the process and often come in waves. Rather than rushing into new relationships to avoid discomfort, it's important to pause and tune into what you truly want and need. Taking time for emotional self-awareness sets a strong foundation for healthier and more fulfilling connections down the road.

Rebuilding trust—both in yourself and in others—is key here. Divorce can shake your confidence in love's stability. You might wonder if it's even possible to find happiness again. Trust is not just about believing in someone else's reliability; it's about learning to believe in your own ability to set boundaries, make good choices, and heal. Receiving love starts with giving yourself compassion and recognizing that you deserve respect, kindness, and honesty.

Opening your heart doesn't always mean diving into a romantic relationship immediately. It might mean reconnecting with friends, family, or even developing a new sense of self-love and acceptance. Surrounding yourself with people who support your growth can soften the fear of vulnerability. When your circle nurtures and encourages rather than judges, it creates a safer space to rediscover trust and intimacy. Those relationships can serve as practice grounds for opening up emotionally, without the pressure or risks of romance.

Many who have lived through the end of a marriage wrestle with doubts about love itself. "Will I ever truly love again?" "Is it worth the risk?" Those questions are valid and deserve thoughtful reflection. Understand that your capacity to love has not been diminished by loss; it's been reshaped by experience. Your heart carries wisdom now—wisdom about what you value, what hurts you, and what you need to feel truly seen and safe. Approaching new love from a place of self-awareness and healing also increases the chance of healthier, more balanced relationships that honor who you've become.

It's natural to worry about repeating old patterns. Perhaps you've identified where the past relationship went wrong, and that awareness can guide your choices moving forward. But remember, no two relationships are the same. Each connection is a fresh chance to build on new understandings and strengths.

Trusting yourself to set boundaries and recognize red flags is essential. Your past experience gives you a kind of emotional radar—one that helps protect your well-being. Opening your heart cautiously, not guardedly, means balancing hope with wisdom. It means giving yourself grace to move forward, without rushing or forcing the process.

Patience with yourself is crucial too. Love after loss doesn't follow a timeline. For some, the readiness to date or engage in new relationships comes sooner; for others, it may take months or even years. Neither is right or wrong. What matters most is honoring where you are emotionally and respecting your pace without judgment. The goal is true healing and authentic connection, not checking off boxes or meeting expectations.

In this journey of opening your heart again, forgiveness plays a powerful role as well. Forgiving doesn't mean excusing what caused pain or pretending everything's fine. It means freeing yourself from the chains of resentment that keep you stuck in the past. As you let go of bitterness, your heartroom expands naturally, making space for new experiences and feelings. Forgiveness offers peace and opens paths to personal freedom that are necessary before embracing new love.

There's also a kind of strength that comes from vulnerability. Sharing your story, your fears, and your hopes with someone new can be terrifying, but it deepens connection. When you're honest about your journey, you invite trust and authenticity. Choosing to open your heart again is an act of bravery—a decision to believe in the possibility of joy despite previous heartbreak.

Reentering the dating world—or even simply opening yourself to love's potential—can be daunting. The post-divorce landscape looks different, and so do your needs. Honoring this shift means redefining what love looks like for you now. It isn't about recreating the past but forging something that fits your transformed self. Love after loss can be gentler, wiser, and more aligned with your true values.

Sometimes, love after loss shows up in unexpected ways. It might be a renewed friendship, a new passion, or a deeper sense of self-acceptance that changes how you relate to others. Being open means staying curious and flexible, willing to embrace whatever form love takes as you grow.

Ultimately, opening your heart again is about reclaiming your story as the author of your life. Divorce may have forced you to rewrite large parts of your narrative, but love offers a chance to craft new chapters filled with possibility. It's an invitation to rediscover hope, joy, and connection on your own terms.

This journey won't always be easy, but it's profoundly rewarding. You don't have to carry the weight of your past forever. You can choose to let your heart heal, expand, and bloom anew.

Remember that love after loss begins internally, with kindness toward yourself and a willingness to embrace the unknown. Take small steps. Trust in your resilience. The promise of new joy waits just beyond the horizon, ready to welcome you when you choose to open your heart once more.

Should You Date Again? Making the Choice

Deciding whether to date again after a divorce isn't a simple yes-or-no question. It's deeply personal and often tangled up in a mix of emotions—from hope and fear to excitement and hesitation. The end of a marriage can leave you wondering if it's even possible to open your heart again, or if you should first dedicate time to simply rediscovering who you are on your own. There's no universal timeline or straightforward rulebook; instead, this choice calls for empathy toward yourself, honesty about your needs, and clarity about your readiness.

The first thing to remember is that dating isn't a mandatory step in healing. It's perfectly okay to take more time than you think you should. Sometimes the pressure to "get back out there" comes from others, or even your own sense of loneliness, rather than a genuine place of readiness. If you're still wrestling with feelings of anger, sadness, or confusion, jumping into a new relationship might cloud your judgment or prolong your healing process. It's important to ask: Are you seeking connection with another person, or are you trying to fill a void left by your divorce?

On the other hand, dating can be a courageous act of reclaiming joy and reaffirming your ability to love and be loved. When approached thoughtfully, it can lead to renewed self-confidence and new discoveries about yourself. But how do you know when it's the right time? One helpful way is to check in with your emotional landscape. If you feel stable enough to engage vulnerably with someone else—without expecting them to fix your pain or complete your identity—that's a promising sign. Healthy dating starts from a place of self-awareness and self-respect.

It's essential to consider what you want before diving back into the dating scene. Are you looking for a serious relationship, casual companionship, or simply some safe social interactions? Being clear with yourself helps set boundaries and avoid misunderstandings later. You might find that your desires have shifted in ways that surprise you since your divorce. Perhaps you want to date more mindfully this time—slowing down and truly connecting rather than rushing into something. There's value in pacing yourself and honoring your unique path.

Taking stock of your self-worth is another crucial aspect of this decision. After a divorce, many people struggle with feelings of inadequacy or question their desirability. It's important to remind yourself that your value isn't tied to your relationship status. Dating should come from a place of self-love—where you're not seeking validation, but rather companionship that complements your already rich life. When you approach dating with this mindset, you're more likely to attract relationships that uplift and respect you.

Fear often lurks beneath the surface when contemplating new romantic connections. Fear of rejection, fear of repeating past mistakes, or fear of opening up and getting hurt again.

These fears are natural. Healing doesn't mean erasing them overnight, but rather learning how to face them without letting them dictate your choices. Acting from fear can keep you stuck, while acting from courage—even if you feel unsure—can open doors to meaningful experiences.

It can also help to look back at your divorce not as a failure, but as a tough chapter that shaped you. What lessons have you taken from it? How have you grown? Understanding this can clarify what you want—and don't want—in future relationships. For instance, you may realize that healthy communication or shared values matter more now than before. Knowing what you need keeps you aligned with your evolving self and helps you avoid repeating patterns that didn't serve you well before.

In practical terms, consider how dating might fit into your current life. If you're managing kids, work, or other responsibilities, finding time and energy for new relationships isn't always easy. Being realistic about your schedule and emotional bandwidth prevents you from feeling overwhelmed or guilty about dividing attention. Remember, dating should enhance your life, not complicate it.

Another critical point is to be mindful of the emotional baggage you may still carry. It's normal to have lingering feelings about your ex, or unresolved grief that creeps up at unexpected moments. Before dating, it's worth taking a pause to confront these emotions—through journaling, therapy, or conversations with trusted friends. Entering a relationship without first tending to your inner healing risks bringing old wounds into new situations, which isn't fair to you or your potential partner.

Some people find it helpful to start with low-pressure social interactions rather than formal dating right away. Attending group events, reconnecting with old friends, or engaging in new hobbies can gently expand your social world, allowing you to rebuild confidence in your ability to connect. This approach reduces the pressure and often leads organically to meeting new people without the expectation of romance. When dating eventually becomes a conscious choice, it feels more natural and less like a recovery milestone to check off.

Honesty with potential partners about your divorce and where you are emotionally is another pillar to establishing healthy new relationships. Sharing your story, boundaries, and pace upfront fosters mutual respect and understanding. It also helps weed out those who aren't ready or respectful of your journey. Dating after divorce can feel vulnerable, but it also offers a chance to practice transparency and authenticity—qualities that lay the foundation for more meaningful connections.

Choosing to date again also means being prepared to face setbacks. Not every connection will spark, and some encounters might remind you of past pain. That's a normal part of opening your heart again. Resilience isn't about avoiding discomfort but about moving forward despite it. Give yourself permission to take breaks, reflect, and reset when needed. Healing is not linear, and dating is no exception.

Ultimately, the choice to date or not to date belongs entirely to you. It's your story to rewrite and your chapter to author on your own terms. Whether you step back into the dating world tomorrow or decide to wait months—or even years—that doesn't define your worth or your potential for happiness. What matters most is that the decision feels right for where you are now, honoring your pace, your feelings, and your growth.

Remember, dating after divorce isn't about finding a "fix" for loneliness or pain; it's an opportunity to explore love in a new light. When you make the choice to date again, do it as an empowered person who knows their worth and is ready to engage with openness and intention. And if the choice is to wait longer, trust that time also brings enrichment and clarity. Your journey forward is entirely yours to shape—and every step counts.

What Healthy Love Looks Like Now

After a divorce, the idea of love often feels foreign—like trying to remember a language you once spoke fluently but have since forgotten. Healthy love doesn't look exactly the same as it did before, and that's okay. It evolves because so do you. What once may have felt familiar or even comfortable might now seem restrictive or mismatched with who you are today. The love you build next needs to honor the version of yourself you've reclaimed, the lessons you've learned, and the boundaries you've set.

Healthy love now begins with a clear understanding of your worth and what you deserve. It's not about settling or rushing to fill a void. Instead, it's a partnership rooted in respect, shared values, and mutual growth. There's space for affection, but also for individuality. Unlike past experiences where needs might have been sidelined or overlooked, healthy love today requires that both people feel free to be themselves without fear of judgment or rejection.

One of the biggest shifts you'll notice is how healthy love feels less about dependency and more about choosing each other daily—with clarity and intention. This means you appreciate companionship but don't rely on it to complete you. It values autonomy and recognizes that two whole people coming together creates a stronger bond than when one leans too heavily on the other for identity or happiness. It's a balance that respects space and connection equally.

In the aftermath of divorce, it's natural to fear repeating past mistakes or to carry emotional baggage into new relationships. Healthy love acknowledges these fears but refuses to be controlled by them. It allows vulnerability without risking safety. This kind of love moves forward with cautious optimism, mindful of boundaries, and open communication. Both partners take responsibility for their feelings and actions, fostering trust instead of suspicion or resentment.

Healthy love now is also patient. It understands that healing from divorce takes time and that emotions don't sort themselves out overnight. There's no rush to jump into something serious just for the sake of companionship. Instead, this kind of love moves at a pace that feels right for both people, honoring the need to rebuild individually while exploring connection mutually. For many, this means embracing a season of friendship, learning to enjoy one another's presence without pressure, and letting the relationship develop naturally.

Self-awareness plays a huge role in what healthy love looks like in this new chapter. You're more attuned to your triggers, your patterns, and your needs. This awareness empowers you to speak up for yourself and recognize when something isn't serving your well-being. It helps to spot red flags early on and avoid falling into unhealthy dynamics again. At the same time, it encourages compassion—for yourself and your partner—knowing everyone carries their own history and healing journey.

Another important feature of healthy love after divorce is clear and healthy communication. Gone are the days of assuming your partner will just "get it" or hoping they'll change to fit your expectations. Now, there's a conscious effort to express your feelings and boundaries clearly, while also listening with empathy. Healthy love encourages dialogue that builds connection rather than creating distance or defensiveness. When disagreements come up—as they inevitably will—they're seen as opportunities for growth instead of threats to the relationship's survival.

Respect for boundaries becomes non-negotiable. Whether it's emotional, physical, or practical boundaries, healthy love insists that these be honored consistently. This isn't about building walls but setting clear guidelines that protect both partners' well-being. Boundaries help prevent old wounds from reopening and create a safe, nurturing space where love can thrive. You learn to say no without guilt and to accept no without taking offense—a crucial skill in building lasting, healthy partnerships.

Trust, too, is rebuilt with intention and care. Post-divorce, it's normal to carry suspicion or hesitation around trusting someone new. But healthy love recognizes that trust is earned over time through honesty, consistency, and reliability. It's not blind faith but a series of small, meaningful actions that reinforce safety and confidence in each other. When trust is present, it allows love to deepen beyond surface-level attraction or convenience.

Healthy love now also embraces the idea of partnership as a team effort rather than a one-sided sacrifice. Both people contribute actively to the relationship, from resolving conflicts to supporting each other's ambitions. There's no expectation that one person will carry the other emotionally or financially. Instead, you create a balance of giving and receiving that feels fair and fulfilling. This shared responsibility helps cultivate stability and long-term happiness.

143

Importantly, healthy love honors your life outside the relationship. Your friendships, passions, goals, and self-care routines remain priorities, not afterthoughts. This is a crucial difference from unhealthy relationships where partners might isolate you or expect you to always put them first. Healthy love encourages you to stay connected to who you are and to keep growing as an individual, not losing yourself in the process.

It's also worth noting that healthy love doesn't erase the past—it integrates it. You bring your history, your scars, and your wisdom into new connections with honesty. Instead of hiding or denying your story, you use it as a foundation for deeper understanding and empathy. This openness creates room for genuine intimacy that is both uplifting and resilient.

As much as healthy love is about what you give, it's equally about what you accept. You learn to embrace imperfection—in yourself and in your partner—without settling for disrespect or neglect. You recognize that no one is perfect, but kindness, effort, and alignment in values set the stage for love that lasts.

Ultimately, what healthy love looks like now is a reflection of your growth. It's more mindful, more compassionate, and more rooted in realistic expectations. It blends hope with wisdom, opening your heart without closing your eyes. This new kind of love is not just a fresh chapter; it's a testament to your resilience and commitment to building a life of meaning and joy.

Looking ahead, this foundation of healthy love will empower you to step into relationships with confidence and clarity. You won't settle for less than you deserve, and you'll recognize when something is truly right for you. This discernment is a powerful tool, helping you avoid the pitfalls of the past and embrace connections that support your happiness and growth.

Remember, healthy love now is less about finding "the one" quickly and more about cultivating a relationship that honors where you are in life. There's no perfect timeline, no "right" formula. What matters most is that love respects and reflects the person you've rebuilt—whole, wise, and ready to embrace the next chapter with open arms.

The Power of Forgiveness for Personal Freedom

Forgiveness is often misunderstood. It's not about excusing the wrongs that were done, pretending the pain never happened, or forgetting the lessons learned along the way. Instead, forgiveness is a powerful tool that frees you— from resentment, from anger, and from the emotional chains that hold you back after divorce. When you've been deeply hurt, whether by your ex-partner's actions or the tragic unraveling of what you once thought was forever, forgiving can feel impossible. But choosing to forgive, ultimately, isn't for them; it's for you.

After divorce, it's all too easy to carry around a heavy burden of bitterness. That weight drags down your spirit and clouds your view of the future. You may replay conversations

145

in your mind or obsess over the "what ifs," which can keep you stuck in a painful loop. Forgiveness breaks that cycle. It lets you release those toxic emotions and reclaim your peace of mind. It's a radical act of self-care—an intentional decision to prioritize your emotional freedom over lingering pain.

One of the biggest myths about forgiveness is that it means reconciliation or accepting bad behavior again. That's not the case at all, especially in a post-divorce relationship where maintaining boundaries is essential. Forgiving doesn't mean you have to reconnect or even interact with the person who hurt you. It doesn't require you to minimize your hurt or ignore the impact of their actions. Instead, forgiveness is an internal process, a gift you give yourself so that bitterness doesn't become your permanent companion.

Many who have walked through the dark valley of divorce describe forgiveness as gradual rather than instantaneous. It can't be forced or rushed. Sometimes, it starts as a small glimmer of understanding—a moment where you realize holding onto anger only keeps you trapped. Other times, forgiveness blooms after deep reflection, sometimes helped along by therapy, journaling, or conversations with trusted friends. Whatever pace it takes, it's important to honor where you are in the process without judgment.

It's also crucial to recognize that forgiving yourself plays a significant role here. Divorce often comes with a flood of self-blame, regret, and shame. You might feel like you failed or wonder how you couldn't have made things work. Forgiving yourself means releasing the unrealistic expectations you placed on yourself and acknowledging that everyone's journey includes mistakes and hardships. Self-forgiveness heals the silent wounds that no one else sees but that weigh heavily on your heart.

When you forgive, you break free from the emotional imprisonment of bitterness. Bitterness is deceptively easy to slip into—it disguises itself as justified anger but ultimately deprives you of happiness. It clouds your judgment and can even affect your physical health. Carrying grudges keeps wounds raw and prevents true healing. Forgiveness lets the past be what it is—past—and opens a pathway toward a future defined by peace, clarity, and personal empowerment.

Think about forgiveness as unshackling yourself from invisible chains. Those chains are made from harsh thoughts, endless resentment, or a relentless replay of pain. Each moment spent holding on to rancor is a moment stolen from your joy and personal growth. Granting forgiveness is an act of courage because it means confronting your pain head-on instead of hiding from it. It's saying, "I'm ready to stand in my power, no matter what happened."

It's natural to feel conflicted about forgiveness. You might ask, "How can I forgive someone who hurt me so deeply?" or "Won't forgiving them make me weak?" But forgiving is actually a profound expression of strength. It requires emotional bravery to say, "I choose peace over pain," especially when the hurt goes beyond words. Freedom from past wounds creates space for self-love to grow and helps you redefine your identity beyond victimhood.

In practical terms, forgiveness can transform how you approach your life after divorce. When you free yourself from anger and resentment, you have more energy to focus on rebuilding and rediscovering who you are. Anger blinds you, but forgiveness clears your vision. You find it easier to set healthy boundaries, engage in meaningful relationships, and step forward with confidence. It helps you become the author of your story again, writing chapters of hope rather than chapters shadowed by bitterness.

Forgiveness also reshapes your emotional landscape over time. The grip pain once had loosens, and the scars left behind become reminders of your resilience, not marks of defeat. It allows you to step fully into your new life, unburdened by past injustices. In fact, many who embrace forgiveness after divorce describe a sense of lightness, as if a weight they didn't fully realize they were carrying suddenly lifted.

You don't have to wait for the perfect moment to start forgiving. It's okay if it feels messy or incomplete. Even a small act of forgiveness—like releasing a single hurtful thought or practicing compassion toward yourself—sets the healing process in motion. Think of forgiveness as a muscle that strengthens the more you use it. Each time you choose to forgive, you strengthen your emotional resilience and expand your potential for joy.

It's equally important to recognize that forgiveness doesn't erase accountability. You can forgive without tolerating harmful behavior or dismissing your boundaries. Forgiveness is not a free pass; it's a way to reclaim your power by refusing to let the pain dictate your future. It's an empowering step in releasing the past and stepping into a version of yourself shaped by wisdom rather than wounds.

Ultimately, embracing forgiveness after divorce leads to a renewed sense of personal freedom. It's a gift that keeps giving because it allows you to live authentically and fully, unhampered by bitterness or resentment. You don't trade away your hurt—you acknowledge it, learn from it, and let it go. In that release, you find peace and the courage to move forward with hope and purpose.

Forgiveness is a choice. It's not always easy, but it's one of the most transformative choices you can make. It paves the way for healing, growth, and a deeper connection with yourself. When you choose to forgive, you're not only rewriting your story—you're reclaiming your life.

Letting Go of Bitterness for You, Not Them

One of the heaviest burdens you can carry after a divorce is bitterness. It sneaks in quietly, sometimes disguised as justified anger or righteous indignation, and over time, it can shape the way you see yourself and the world around you. But here's the truth: holding onto bitterness doesn't punish the person who hurt you—it only weighs you down. Letting go of that bitterness is an act of kindness and strength you owe yourself, not an act of forgiveness for anyone else.

Bitterness feels like armor, right? It's easy to mistake it for protection because it puts you in a defensive stance, ready to fend off more pain. But what it really does is trap you in a cycle of negative emotions that keep your heart closed to healing and new beginnings. When you're bitter, it's as if you're dragging around a heavy load of old wounds every day—java anchors that slow your pace and cloud your perspective. It's exhausting, but letting go can feel just as daunting because it means stepping into vulnerability again. Still, freeing yourself from bitterness isn't about forgetting what happened or pretending the pain wasn't real. It's about choosing peace over poison.

Think about bitterness as a chain linking you to the past, a past that no longer serves your future. Every time you replay the wrongs, every time you wish things were different or someone else had acted another way, you're strengthening that chain. Breaking free means understanding that your healing is your priority. Your ex's choices don't have to define you. When you decide to release bitterness, you reclaim control over your emotions and your story. You stop letting resentment dictate your happiness or stand in the way of your growth.

It's important to remind yourself that letting go isn't the same as excusing behavior that hurt you. You don't have to forget or condone what was done. Instead, you're choosing to no longer let those memories poison your present. This reframing is incredibly powerful because it shifts your mindset from victimhood to empowerment. And empowerment is the fuel you need to rewrite your story—

instead of being stuck, you get to start crafting a life that's richer, freer, and joyful.

It's normal to feel that bitterness has a purpose at first. It validates your pain and makes your suffering visible, especially after a breakup where feelings were complex and wounds ran deep. But clinging too long to these feelings only delays your healing. Bitterness acts like a wall between you and peace. With each day that passes focusing on what went wrong or who's to blame, the wall grows taller. Eventually, it becomes harder to see past it to the opportunities and happiness waiting on the other side. Choosing to let go means deciding to tear down that wall.

Starting this process takes courage because bitterness often disguises itself as loyalty—to your pain, your experience, or your sense of justice. It's tempting to hold tight to your anger because it feels like proof you're still "right" in some way. But the truth of moving on is that there's strength in release. It's not weakness to set your bitterness aside; it's a sign that you're ready to live unshackled. You get to stop investing your energy in things that don't build you up. Instead, you choose to invest in your own freedom and happiness.

Part of letting go involves practicing self-compassion. You might have moments when reminiscence triggers anger or resentment, and that's okay. Being gentle with yourself through these ups and downs is key. It helps you to remember that healing is nonlinear. Bitterness can resurface unexpectedly, but with time, you'll find these moments become fewer and less intense. Each small act of kindness toward yourself chips away at old pain and gently reshapes your inner landscape.

In practical terms, letting go often means creating boundaries with people or situations that stir up bitterness. That could mean limiting contact with your ex, avoiding conversations that dig up old wounds, or steering clear of social media reminders. Protecting your emotional space is vital. It helps you to focus on what nourishes your spirit instead of what drains it. Sometimes, physical distance is necessary to maintain mental and emotional distance, giving you room to breathe and heal.

Another useful strategy is to redirect your energy toward something meaningful—activities or projects that inspire you or bring you joy. When your focus shifts from bitterness to growth, you build a new part of yourself that stands firmly in the present rather than the past. This could be picking up a hobby you abandoned, dedicating time to friends and family, or setting new personal goals. These outlets encourage positive emotions and reinforce that your life is not defined by loss but by potential.

Forgiveness is often misunderstood as forgetting or reconciling, but in reality, it is a personal liberation. When you're ready, forgiving feels less like a gift to the other person and more like a release valve for the pressure you've felt inside. It's the moment you choose to stop being controlled by your pain and to step into your own power. This type of forgiveness doesn't have a timeline—you come to it in your own time, at your own pace. There's no rush and no judgment if you're not there yet.

Remember, bitterness stands between you and your future self. It keeps you locked in a chapter of your life when you want to be writing the next one. Your healing journey is about taking back your narrative to focus on who you want to be, not who you were forced to be. Your past does not have to dictate your value or your ability to find joy. Letting go of bitterness opens the door to peace, hope, and the freedom to build a life on your own terms.

In the end, the choice to surrender bitterness is one of the most powerful tools in rewriting your story. It's about choosing peace instead of pain, growth instead of grudges, and love—especially for yourself—above all else. You owe it to yourself to carry only what helps you move forward. The rest is simply unnecessary weight, and it's time to leave it behind.

How to Move Forward with Peace and Purpose

Moving forward after divorce isn't about rushing to the next chapter but stepping into it with intention. The path ahead can feel uncertain, but peace and purpose don't have to be strangers to your post-divorce life. In fact, they're the compass that will help you navigate this new terrain with strength—and perhaps even grace. Peace isn't just the absence of conflict or pain; it's a conscious choice to find calm within yourself, despite the storms that life throws your way. Purpose, on the other hand, is that deeper feeling that

153

what you're doing matters and that you're moving toward something meaningful, not just drifting aimlessly.

It's natural that right now you might feel torn between holding on to what was and stepping fully into what could be. But here's the thing: peace and purpose grow when you stop fighting against your current reality and begin working with it. That means accepting where you are emotionally, mentally, and even physically, without judgment. It means giving yourself permission to release old resentments and regrets that no longer serve you. By doing so, you create the space in your heart and mind for genuine healing and a renewed sense of direction.

Finding peace starts with self-compassion. It's easy to be your own harshest critic, especially when rebuilding your confidence and self-worth after divorce. But ever wonder how different life would feel if you treated yourself as kindly as you would a close friend dealing with the same situation? When you practice kindness toward yourself, it softens the weight of pain and disappointment. It invites patience into your healing process, reminding you that just like any chapter of growth, this phase takes time. You don't have to have it all figured out right now. Peace grows little by little, through everyday moments of self-care, positive affirmation, and self-forgiveness.

Purpose follows peace in a very natural way. When you come into harmony with your present self, you can begin to tune into what truly matters to you beyond the circumstances of your divorce. What dreams or goals have you tucked away? What values light a fire in your heart? Embracing purpose means reconnecting with those pieces of yourself that may have been dimmed or overlooked. You don't have to start with a grand plan. Sometimes purpose shows up in the simple commitment to take small actions that align with who you want to become. Those steps build momentum and cultivate a renewed sense of meaning in your daily life.

Remember, moving forward with peace and purpose isn't about forgetting the past or pretending everything is perfect. It's about making peace with your story so far and using that understanding to fuel your new beginning. Sometimes, that requires revisiting old wounds in a way that's gentle yet honest. It might look like reflecting on what lessons your experience has taught you or recognizing patterns you want to break free from. This isn't easy work, but it's incredibly freeing. It opens the door to rewriting your narrative not as a victim of divorce, but as a survivor and a creator of your own future.

One of the biggest obstacles to peace is often your inner dialogue. Divorce can leave you wrestling with an ongoing mental loop of what went wrong or self-blame. Peace requires changing that conversation. It means consciously shifting your focus from criticism to curiosity. Instead of asking why things fell apart or what you did wrong, you can ask, "What can I learn from this?" or "How can I grow from this experience?" This subtle change lays the groundwork for personal empowerment, which naturally leads to a stronger sense of purpose.

It's also important to recognize that peace and purpose don't mean doing everything alone. Healing is not a solo journey, even if parts of it feel deeply personal. You're allowed—and encouraged—to seek support. Whether it's friends, family, a therapist, or community groups, connecting with others who understand your experience can be transformative. Shared stories and empathy remind you that you're not isolated in your feelings or challenges, and that collective strength can inspire your individual peace and purpose.

Setting boundaries is another key to moving forward healthily. Divorce often blurs lines that once kept you feeling safe and centered. Reasserting your boundaries protects your energy and nurtures your peace. This might mean limiting contact with people or situations that trigger old wounds or withholding your time and emotional energy from anything that doesn't align with your well-being. Boundaries say to yourself, "I am worthy of respect and peace." They create the mental and emotional space needed for you to focus on what truly serves your growth.

While many view moving forward as something linear, it's usually more of a winding road. Some days you'll feel strength and clarity; other days, you might feel lost or overwhelmed. Both are part of moving forward with peace and purpose. Giving yourself permission to experience the full range of feelings—without judgment or rush—is vital. Healing doesn't always look like a steady climb; sometimes it's a series of small steps and pauses, visits to the past, and moments of quiet reflection. This ebb and flow actually mirrors real life and holds space for authentic transformation.

One practical way to cultivate peace and purpose is through setting clear, manageable goals. These don't have to be huge life changes. Sometimes, simply committing to daily habits that nourish your mind and body—like a morning walk, journaling, or quiet meditation—can ground you and signal your intent to move forward. As confidence grows, you can begin to layer in bigger aspirations. Goals give your purpose direction and measurable milestones. Celebrating small successes reinforces your belief in yourself and helps maintain motivation when the road gets tough.

It's okay—and even necessary—to redefine what success and happiness mean to you now. Divorce changes the parameters of your life, but it also opens opportunities to rediscover what feels fulfilling. Maybe that means exploring new hobbies, investing in friendships, or pursuing work or education that excites you. Purpose blossoms when your actions align with your values and passions. As you rewrite your story, allow yourself to dream in fresh ways, without old constraints or doubts holding you back.

Moving forward with peace and purpose also includes embracing forgiveness—not necessarily for others, but first for yourself. Holding onto bitterness or regrets only ties you to pain. Forgiving yourself for perceived mistakes or for not having all the answers frees you to fully step into the life you are creating. Forgiveness is sometimes misunderstood as forgetting or excusing hurtful actions; instead, it's about releasing your emotional grip on those experiences so they don't dictate your future.

Finally, recognize that peace and purpose are active states, not passive ones. They require daily choice and commitment, even when it's challenging. This doesn't mean forcing happiness or pretending pain doesn't exist. It means choosing to engage with your healing intentionally and using each day as an opportunity to live closer to your truth. You are building a foundation of resilience, and that inner strength is what will carry you through not just this transition, but all the chapters that follow.

There is profound power in knowing that you are authoring your own comeback story. Divorce may have marked an ending, but it's also the beginning of rewriting your life with new peace and purpose. You're learning how to honor your past while stepping courageously into a future crafted by your own dreams and decisions. This journey isn't always easy, but it's yours—and it holds the potential for profound growth, deep healing, and radiant joy.

Your Comeback Story: Embracing Resilience

Divorce shakes the foundation of everything you once knew. It cracks open your world and forces you to face a reality that wasn't part of your original plan. But embedded in that upheaval, there lies something powerful—a chance to rise, stronger and more resilient than ever before. This is your comeback story, the chapter where you finally embrace resilience as more than just a word but as a way of life.

Resilience isn't about pretending everything's okay when it's not. It's not about putting on a brave face or swallowing your pain silently. It's about recognizing your wounds, feeling the depth of your losses, and still choosing to move forward. It's a process — sometimes slow, often messy — but always worthwhile. Embracing resilience means accepting that life has thrown you a curveball, and rather than giving up, you're ready to catch it and throw it right back.

In the aftermath of divorce, it's easy to dwell on what you've lost—the shared dreams, the daily routines, the future you imagined. But resilience calls for a shift in perspective. What if you saw this moment not as the end of your story, but as a hard reset? When you let go of what was, you create space for what can be. This mindset isn't natural for most people. It requires practice, patience, and sometimes the kind of stubborn hope that refuses to be extinguished no matter how dark the nights get.

One of the first steps toward resilience is reclaiming your sense of self. Divorce often feels like a losing battle for identity, especially if your self-worth was intertwined with your role as a spouse. But remember, your identity wasn't lost when your marriage ended—it was buried under layers of grief, fear, and uncertainty. Resilience helps you dig through those layers, rediscovering the core of who you are beyond the labels and expectations. This process may stir up feelings of loneliness or confusion, but it also opens the door to incredible personal growth.

Embracing resilience means showing up for yourself even on the days you don't feel like it. Some days, you'll feel like falling apart—and that's okay. The point isn't to never break down but to build the muscle that lets you get back up each time you do. Think of resilience as a kind of emotional fitness. The more you practice self-compassion, set healthy boundaries, and take deliberate steps toward healing, the stronger you become. It's a daily commitment to yourself, even when progress feels invisible.

The power of resilience also lies in how it transforms your relationship with pain. Divorce hurts—there's no way around it. But pain becomes less of a prison when you start to see it as a fuel for change. This isn't about glorifying suffering or pretending it's a gift. Instead, it's about harnessing that discomfort to propel you forward. Pain sharpens your clarity, revealing what truly matters and what you're willing to fight for—your happiness, your freedom, your peace.

Many people imagine resilience as a solo journey, but it rarely is. Community and connection play an essential role in bouncing back. Whether it's leaning on friends, finding support groups, or seeking guidance from a therapist, reaching out doesn't make you weak—it makes you human. Resilience grows when you let others in, borrow strength from shared experiences, and realize you're far from alone. In fact, those connections often become vital pillars in rebuilding your life.

At the heart of your comeback story is the idea that setbacks don't define you; your response to them does. Resilience means rewriting the narrative you tell yourself about divorce. Instead of a story filled with regret or shame, you craft one of courage and empowerment. You become the protagonist who faced unimaginable challenges and came through with new wisdom, confidence, and self-love. Every small victory, from choosing gratitude to setting a boundary, is a chapter in that unfolding story.

As you embrace resilience, you'll notice a subtle shift in how you view your future. The uncertainty won't disappear overnight, but hope starts to take root. You begin to trust that you're capable of creating a life filled with joy, stability, and meaning—even if it looks different than what you imagined before. This faith in the future is not naive optimism but a hard-earned belief born from surviving hardship and choosing to thrive anyway.

It's also important to recognize that resilience doesn't mean rushing your healing or forcing yourself to "move on" on society's timeline. There's no finish line or perfect moment when pain suddenly turns into peace. Instead, resilience wends its way through your experience like a steady current, sometimes strong, sometimes gentle but always persistent. Allow yourself to feel what needs to be felt, cry when necessary, and celebrate progress no matter how small. This balance is what nurtures true resilience—grit wrapped in grace.

Another vital element of resilience in your comeback story is reclaiming your voice. Divorce can silence you in many ways—through self-doubt, social stigma, or the overwhelming flood of emotions. But resilience empowers

FINDING YOURSELF AFTER DIVORCE

you to speak your truth again. You learn to articulate your needs, desires, and boundaries clearly and without apology. This act of self-expression isn't just liberating; it's foundational to rebuilding your sense of self and your relationships with others.

Many who have faced divorce have told me that resilience showed up unexpectedly—during moments they least expected. It might be getting through a tough conversation without falling apart or deciding to try something new even though fear screamed at them to stay put. These small acts of courage steadily accumulate, weaving a tapestry of strength and perseverance. Your comeback story will look unique because it's threaded with your own experiences, your own lessons, and your own brand of resilience.

Along the way, you may discover new passions, hobbies, or purposes that were buried beneath the weight of your previous life. Resilience invites curiosity and adventure even in the face of uncertainty. It challenges you to explore who you are now, without judgment or comparison. This exploration is not a distraction—it's an essential part of your healing and rebirth. Each new discovery brings you closer to a vibrant, empowered version of yourself that's ready to embrace the next chapter.

Embracing resilience means also forgiving yourself. Divorce can leave you carrying heavy burdens of guilt, shame, or regret. Letting go of these weights doesn't happen all at once, but resilience asks you to give yourself permission to heal one step at a time. Forgiveness becomes a gift you give to yourself, freeing you from the chains of past mistakes or perceived failures. This freedom is crucial because it clears the space for hope, joy, and renewed confidence to grow.

As your comeback story unfolds, you'll realize that resilience isn't just about surviving—it's about thriving. It means finding beauty in your scars and strength in your scars. You become a living testament to what's possible when pain meets courage. Every day you choose to rise despite the odds, you send a message to yourself: your story isn't over. It's just getting started.

This journey isn't easy, and you won't always get it right. There will be moments when the past calls louder than the future, when the wounds feel fresh, and when doubts creep in. But resilience is the quiet voice inside that says, "Keep going." It's the determination to write your own ending, with hope and power as your guides. Your comeback story is waiting. Embrace it with open arms, knowing that resilience has already been growing within you all along.

Turning Pain into Purpose and Empowerment

Divorce often leaves a deep ache—something so raw it feels unbearable at times. But what if that pain, as tough as it is, could become the very fuel that ignites your next chapter? The journey from heartbreak to hope is rarely linear; it twists and turns, but on the other side lies a chance not just to survive, but to thrive. Turning pain into purpose isn't about erasing the hurt; it's about channeling it into something meaningful.

When your world feels like it's been shattered, the instinct is often to hide away, to shrink from the world and protect what's left of your heart. And that's okay—giving yourself permission to feel hurt and vulnerable is essential. But at some point, holding onto that pain without transforming it can keep you stuck in a painful loop. That transformation starts by recognizing that your story doesn't end with your divorce. It evolves. And within that evolution lies power.

Many people find that the struggle itself gifts unexpected insights about their inner strength. Pain sharpens self-awareness. You begin to see what really matters to you, not what others wanted for you or what was dictated by your old life. This isn't about flipping a switch and suddenly feeling whole again; it's about small moments of clarity that build over time. It's in these moments you discover your capacity to redefine your worth and rebuild your life on your terms.

Empowerment begins with reclaiming control— something that often feels lost amid the chaos of divorce. You might have faced countless "what ifs" and "should haves," but they don't have to dictate where you're headed. Taking ownership of your healing journey means choosing how you respond to your experiences. You have the power to rewrite the narrative, moving from victim to survivor to thriver. This shift isn't just motivational talk; it's a real, tangible process of redirecting your energy.

Purpose, meanwhile, starts with a simple question: What do I want my life to stand for moving forward? It's easy to focus on the loss—on endings and what went wrong.

But purpose asks you to look ahead, inviting you to create a vision centered around your values and passions. Maybe it's investing time in relationships that uplift you, or pursuing a career change that excites you. Whatever it is, purpose gives your journey meaning beyond the pain.

One powerful way to channel pain into purpose is to see your experience as part of a bigger story—your story. Every setback and heartbreak has shaped you into who you are now. That doesn't minimize the hardships you've faced, but it does honor your resilience. It's about embracing the truth that your life's narrative is far from over. In fact, this chapter can be one of the richest and most transformative.

The transformation often starts by shifting your mindset. Instead of asking "Why did this happen to me?" try asking, "What is this teaching me?" This change in perspective is subtle but monumental. It doesn't erase the pain or deny the injustice—you're simply opening the door to growth and learning. It's an active choice to find meaning, even if the road to that meaning takes time and patience.

Empowerment also comes from setting new boundaries and priorities. After divorce, you may have felt that your needs and desires were sidelined for too long. Now is the time to say yes to yourself unapologetically. This might look like saying no to toxic relationships, committing to your own self-care routines, or cultivating friendships and communities that support your well-being. These choices build a foundation of strength from which you can confidently move forward.

Another aspect of turning pain into empowerment is embracing vulnerability. It's tempting to guard your heart fiercely after loss, but vulnerability doesn't signify weakness. Instead, it opens the door to genuine connection and healing. When you allow yourself to be seen—even the parts bruised by divorce—you reclaim your authenticity. This authenticity is a potent form of power because it fosters real intimacy, both with yourself and others.

Purpose and empowerment also thrive when you celebrate small victories. Maybe you've taken the first steps to pursue a dream you shelved years ago or finally set healthy boundaries with family members. Each of these moments, while seemingly minor, signals growth and movement. Acknowledging progress creates momentum, reminding you that you're not stuck—you're evolving.

Remember, empowerment isn't about rushing to "fix" everything or erasing your emotions. It's about learning to walk alongside your feelings, letting them fuel your transformation without drowning you. Pain is a signal, an invitation to pay attention and care for yourself differently. When you honor that signal, you're already reclaiming your power.

It's also important to recognize you don't have to do this alone. Seeking support—whether through therapy, support groups, or trusted friends—can deepen your journey from pain to empowerment. Healing communities provide perspective and solidarity, reminding you that pain is universal but so is resilience. No one's comeback story is written in isolation.

In many cases, the purpose that arises out of pain extends beyond just personal healing. Some find themselves drawn to help others navigating similar struggles. Whether you become a mentor, an advocate, or simply a compassionate listener, transforming your pain into purpose can build connection and meaning that reaches far beyond yourself.

The heart of this process lies in permission—permission to redefine your identity, to live boldly, and to dream again. Divorce can feel like an ending, but it can also be a powerful beginning. You're not just recovering from loss; you're crafting a life driven by your own values, dreams, and newfound strength.

Every step you take to turn your pain into purpose is a statement that your story isn't defined by heartbreak. It's defined by your courage to rise, to rebuild, and to choose joy and fulfillment. That's the essence of empowerment. It's not about forgetting what's happened; it's about using that experience as a launching pad.

As you continue writing your next chapter, hold onto this truth: the pain you've endured is real and valid, but it doesn't have the final say. You do. And that choice—to turn pain into purpose and empowerment—is among the most powerful choices you can make.

You Are the Author Now: Writing Your Next Chapter

By the time you reach this point in your journey, you've weathered many storms. You've faced the pain, reclaimed your identity, and started rebuilding your life with intention. Now, the most exciting part begins: realizing that you hold the pen to your own story. The past may have written chapters filled with heartbreak and hardship, but your future is an open book. This is your moment to write what comes next, on your own terms.

It's empowering to understand that the next chapter isn't about erasing everything that came before—it's about integrating all your experiences, lessons learned, and newfound strength to create a narrative that reflects who you truly are now and who you want to become. Divorce is a powerful punctuation mark, an end that signals a new beginning rather than a full stop. You have the right to decide what themes and characters fill this next section of your life.

One of the first things to embrace is the idea of self-authorship. Nobody else gets to decide your story anymore. No matter the opinions or judgments of others, you're the one who knows your truth best. This clarity brings freedom. With it, you can start dreaming bigger and clearer, casting aside doubts rooted in your past. Whatever your goals—whether it's career growth, emotional healing, new relationships, or simply reclaiming joy—you now have the power to set your path without hesitation or hesitation.

Writing your own chapter means being intentional about the direction you want to move in. That might look like setting bold new goals in areas of your life that felt stagnant or overshadowed by the divorce. Perhaps you've discovered passions or talents you'd set aside, and now they're calling you forward. Or maybe this is the time to redefine what happiness means to you, on a much deeper level, beyond external validation or previous definitions tied to your marriage.

At the same time, it's important to honor the vulnerability this stage can bring. Starting fresh isn't always comfortable. It asks for bravery—that willingness to step into the unknown with an open heart. It means accepting that you might stumble or change your mind, and that's perfectly okay. Growth often looks messy. It requires patience and kindness toward yourself as you navigate this uncharted territory. There's no perfect way to do this; just your way.

Creating your next chapter also demands that you shed any lingering voices of doubt or defeat. Those internal critics that whisper "you're not enough" or "it's too late to change" need to be challenged and quieted. You've already proven your resilience. This book you're writing is a testament to that resilience, a story of survival that naturally evolves into one of hope and strength. Let your inner voice be one of encouragement and affirmation. Speak to yourself as you would a friend who's deserving of love and respect.

Remember, this chapter is yours to customize. You can choose the pace, the tone, and the characters who enter your story moving forward. You might welcome new friendships or nurture old ones that support your growth. You might step into self-care routines that feed your spirit or explore activities that awaken your sense of joy. Every choice you make is a line written with intention and care.

This stage of rewriting your story isn't just about surviving—it's about thriving in ways you never thought possible. It's about creating meaning from the ashes of what was lost. Turning pain into purpose becomes a powerful tool here. When you view your past challenges as the foundation for your next successes and joys, your story becomes rich with depth and authenticity.

It's helpful to view your story as a living, breathing project—always in progress and open to adjustments. You aren't locked into a rigid script. If a particular chapter doesn't feel right, you can revise, rewrite, or even start fresh. This flexibility grants you daily permission to evolve without guilt or pressure. Life after divorce is not a linear path; it's a winding road you get to navigate with courage.

One of the most transformative acts you can embrace in writing your next chapter is forgiveness. Forgiveness—whether of yourself or others—doesn't mean forgetting or excusing what happened. Instead, it's a conscious choice to release yourself from the weight of bitterness and anger, freeing up space for peace and new beginnings. Carrying resentment only drags you back when your goal is forward motion. Letting go becomes a gift you give yourself.

With forgiveness and self-compassion, your narrative can become one of empowerment. You're not just the author—you're also the protagonist who grows stronger, more resilient, and more confident with every page you turn. Imagine the story you'd be proud to read years from now. What lessons would you want yourself to know? What victories would you celebrate? What joys would you savor? Hold those visions close as guiding stars.

As you start putting words down on the pages of your new chapter, don't shy away from celebrating the small wins along the way. Each moment of courage, each decision to prioritize yourself, each day you move through post-divorce life with grace, is a building block of something greater. Writing your next chapter involves acknowledging those moments, knowing they are the proof of your progress.

Stepping fully into the role of author means claiming your narrative authority with confidence and compassion. It invites you to be proactive in shaping your story rather than simply reacting to life's events. This mindset shifts you from feeling like life is happening to you, to you actively crafting the experience of your life. That's an incredibly powerful place to be.

Lastly, keep in mind that this chapter is not just a solitary journey. Though you are the author, you aren't alone. Seek out allies and communities that support your growth and celebrate your evolution. Surrounding yourself with encouragement and understanding not only bolsters your confidence, but also enriches your story with connections that nurture your heart and soul.

So, with your pen in hand, know that the pages ahead are blank for a reason. Filled with possibility, ripe for transformation, and waiting for the unique story only you can tell. Embrace the opportunity to shape a future filled with resilience, joy, and newfound freedom. The author inside you is ready to write the next chapter—boldly, beautifully, and unapologetically.

Conclusion

Walking through the aftermath of divorce is rarely easy, but it also marks the beginning of a profound transformation. What felt like an ending really becomes a powerful opening—a chance to reclaim your story and rebuild your life from the ground up. This journey may test you in ways you never imagined, yet it's also rich with opportunities to discover strength, rediscover joy, and redefine what happiness means to you. Though the road can be winding, every step forward is a victory in itself.

It's important to remember that healing is not linear. Some days will feel like progress, while others might pull you back into old feelings of loss or frustration. That's natural and okay. What matters most is showing up for yourself with kindness and patience, no matter where you find yourself emotionally. The tough days don't erase the growth you're making; rather, they often deepen your resilience and capacity for empathy, both toward yourself and others.

At the core of moving forward is reclaiming your identity beyond the labels and roles that divorce may have disrupted. It's a messy, beautiful process of peeling back layers to expose the truest version of you—someone who isn't defined by past circumstances but by your values, passions, and authentic voice. This rediscovery can light a new kind of fire inside, inspiring you to pursue dreams that might have been shelved or unnoticed before.

The power you hold in shaping your future can sometimes be underestimated. Divorce shifts the playing field, but it also puts agency firmly in your hands. You get to decide what comes next, whether that means focusing on personal growth, nurturing relationships that uplift you, or building a life filled with purpose and intention. Trusting yourself in making these choices is key, even when the path ahead is unclear. Confidence, after all, grows through action—sometimes small steps taken consistently over time.

Part of this empowerment comes from releasing old narratives that no longer serve you. Divorce can bring with it feelings of guilt, shame, or bitterness, but holding onto those emotions only weighs you down. Forgiveness—whether for yourself or for others—is not about excusing hurtful behavior; it's about freeing yourself from the chains of resentment. When you make space for peace, you open yourself to new possibilities that resentment would have blocked.

Every story includes moments of vulnerability and strength, and your journey through divorce is no different. Learning to be gentle with your heart while pushing forward requires balance. Practicing self-compassion is not weakness; it's a courageous act of acknowledging your struggles while affirming your worth. The more you nurture this relationship with yourself, the stronger your foundation becomes as you build anew.

Building a fresh life also means allowing yourself to dream again—and this time, on your own terms. The freedom to envision what brings you fulfillment can be exhilarating and daunting all at once, but don't shy away from it. Whether your focus is career, relationships, hobbies, or personal growth, exploring new possibilities breathes life into the future you're creating. Give yourself permission to be hopeful, ambitious, and even a little daring.

For those navigating co-parenting or caring for children through these changes, your strength and compassion create a ripple effect beyond your own healing. Modeling resilience and emotional maturity to your children sets an empowering example they'll carry forward. It's one of the toughest roles post-divorce, yet it is also one of the most impactful— showing your family that love and stability exist in new forms and that life's challenges can be met with grace and intention.

The journey you've taken has likely brought you through moments of deep pain and immense growth. It's worth honoring both, without minimizing either. Pain doesn't signal failure—and growth doesn't mean forgetting what you've experienced. Your story is richer and more textured because of it. Embracing this complexity allows you to step into your next chapter with authenticity and courage, ready to live a life that feels truly your own.

Ultimately, this chapter in your life is about crafting your own narrative—a narrative rooted in resilience, self-love, and purpose. You are not merely surviving divorce;

you're transforming through it. The lessons learned, the strength gained, and the new dreams sparked along the way all become chapters in the story you get to tell, one filled with hope, empowerment, and peace.

Take heart in knowing that you are not alone on this path. Many have walked it before you, and many will follow. There is power in connection, community, and shared experience, even if your journey feels uniquely yours. Reaching out when you need support, embracing moments of joy, and continuing to invest in your healing all contribute to a vibrant, hopeful future.

This is your time to step boldly into the life waiting for you beyond divorce. It won't always be perfect, and that's okay—the beauty lies in the imperfect process, in learning to dance with uncertainty and find joy amid change. Trust yourself to keep moving forward, one step at a time, writing a story that reflects the strength, wisdom, and spirit that make you who you are.

Appendix

This appendix serves as a practical toolkit for you as you continue your journey beyond divorce. Here, you'll find supportive resources, helpful reminders, and actionable tips designed to reinforce the lessons and encouragement shared throughout the book. It's a place to gather strength and clarity when the road gets tough, and to keep your focus steady on healing and growth.

Remember, recovery isn't a linear process, and having easy access to guidance and motivation can make all the difference. This section consolidates tools intended to boost your confidence, offer structure when life feels chaotic, and provide gentle prompts for self-reflection and empowerment.

Whether you're revisiting practices like self-care, exploring new goal-setting ideas, or simply seeking reassurance, the appendix is here to support you as you rebuild your foundation.

Keep in mind that this is your personal roadmap—feel free to adapt these suggestions to what feels right for you. Healing and reinvention happen in your own time and your own way, and these resources are meant to gently nudge you forward, reminding you of the incredible strength already within you.

May this appendix be a quiet companion on your path to rediscovery, offering the encouragement and practical help you deserve as you forge your new life.

www.ingramcontent.com/pod-product-compliance
Lightning Source LLC
Chambersburg PA
CBHW021232090426
42740CB00006B/497

* 9 7 8 1 9 1 8 2 2 3 3 3 0 *